MW00896724

The Laws & Customs of Sukkos
Summary Edition

A digest of laws, customs, Chassidus & Kabala on the Holiday of Sukkos
Based on the rulings of Shulchan Aruch Harav Chapters 625-669 and Chabad
Custom

Summary Edition
The summary provided in this booklet was composed from the upcoming Sefer "The Laws and Customs of Sukkos". The summary does not contain the sources or footnotes, in order to allow for easy flow of the reading. To browse the content of the Sefer online, including footnotes and sources, please visit our website Shulchanaruchharav.com under the Sukkos section, or our future publishing of the full Sefer.

Compiled by: Rabbi Yaakov Goldstein

Shulchanaruchharav.com
Shulchanaruchharav.com is a state of the art Halacha website that contains the largest English database of detailed Halacha available on the web. As part of this site a special Sukkos database has been established to help the learner research any Halacha in Sukkos and have it available on his fingertips. For further information visit our site at www.shulchanaruchharav.com or email us at: rabbi@shulchanaruchharav.com.

Please support us!
Our website is available free of charge and is dependent on Donors like you! Please contact the above email to become a partner in our holy work!

ShulchanAruchHarav.com בס"ד

1. **Largest fully resourced Practical Halacha Database on the web**
2. **Rulings of Alter Rebbe and Chabad custom**
3. **Hundreds of practical Q&A on each subject from the sea of Poskim**
4. **Perfect for the Halachic growth of you and your Ballei Battim**
5. **Daily Halacha video-Register for free**
6. **Weekly Mamar from Torah Or-Register for free**

Halacha Aids   Shabbos Aids   Semicha Aids

1. **Clear, concise, and finely detailed** practical Halacha
2. **Based on Shulchan Aruch Harav & Chabad Custom**

3. **Semicha Aids: Summary of every opinion and Halacha** in the Semicha curriculum! *Perfect for Semicha review!*

Table of Contents

Checklist

The laws of a Kosher Sukkah:

✓ Begin building the Sukkah on Motzei Yom Kippur. Complete the entire Sukkah the day after Yom Kippur, after Shacharis.

✓ Verify that the area you desire to build the Sukkah does not contain any obstructions which will hover over the Sechach of the Sukkah. This includes trees, laundry lines, another neighbors Sechach, etc.

✓ First build at least three complete walls that are ten Tefach high and within three Tefach from the ground and are seven Tefach wide. If using tarp for the walls, make sure to use "Lavud," or to at least tie it very strongly.

✓ Place Kosher Sechach on the walls <u>only after</u> the walls are built.

✓ Don't use Sechach that has bad odor or with leaves that will fall.

✓ Make sure the supports of the Sechach are also Kosher to be used as Sechach. Thus, don't use nails or non-Kosher rope to attach the Sechach.

✓ Make sure to fasten down the Sechach with Kosher material so it does not fly with the wind. One can place a wood board on top of the Sechach and then tie the wood board down with any material.

✓ Verify the Sechach gives majority shade, allows rain and star light to penetrate.

✓ Everyone should try to have their own Sukkah.

✓ Don't build the Sukkah in public property.

✓ Try to personally build the Sukkah versus having someone else do so for you.

✓ Do not have gentiles, women, or children, place the Sechach on the Sukkah. They may however build the walls.

✓ Verify that all pictures and decorations are placed within 4 Tefachim from the Sechach. It is not the Chabad custom to place decorations.

✓ The eating table of the Sukkah must be within the parameters of the Kosher Sukkah.

Leisheiv Basukkah-The Mitzvah of dwelling in a Sukkah:

✓ Each time upon dwelling in the Sukkah have intention to dwell in the Sukkah for the sake of remembering the Exodus and the clouds of glory. The main idea is for one to contemplate this matter.

✓ Male children above the age of 6 are to be educated to dwell in the Sukkah.

✓ Make the Sukkah your permanent residence. This means one must eat, drink, read, learn, socialize, and simply spend time of relaxation [i.e. "Yitayel"] within the Sukkah throughout all seven days, both by night and day.

✓ <u>Eating and drinking in a Sukkah:</u> According to the letter of the law one is only required to eat in the Sukkah if he is eating more than a Kibeitza of bread or Mezonos [within Kdei Achilas Pras]. All foods which do not carry the blessing of Mezonos or Hamotzi may be eaten outside the Sukkah without limitation, even if one sets a meal over those foods. However, one who is stringent to eat even these foods in the Sukkah is praised. The Chabad Minhag is not to eat or drink anything outside the Sukkah, including even water.

✓ <u>Kiddush:</u> Kiddush is to be made inside the Sukkah. The blessing of Leisheiv Basukkah is said prior to drinking the wine. However, on the 1st night of Sukkos it is said before the blessing of Shehechiyanu, while on the 2nd night [in the Diaspora] it is said after the blessing of Shehechiyanu. [During the Kiddush of the day meal, the blessing of Leisheiv is said after the blessing of Hagafen, prior to drinking the wine.]

✓ Havdalah: One is obligated to say Havdalah inside the Sukkah. One says the blessing of Leisheiv Basukkah after Havdalah, prior to drinking from the wine.

✓ Learning in the Sukkah: One must learn Torah inside the Sukkah unless he desires to learn in the Beis Midrash, or to learn outside under fresh air for greater understanding, or he does not have room to store his Sefarim in the Sukkah.

✓ Davening in the Sukkah: One may Daven outside his Sukkah if he desires to Daven in Shul or if he cannot concentrate in the Sukkah.

✓ Sleeping in the Sukkah: It is forbidden to sleep outside of a Sukkah even for a mere nap. The Chabad practice is not to sleep in the Sukkah due to an age-old custom of the Alter Rebbe, and due to the exemption of Mitztaer.

✓ Items to enter into the Sukkah: One should enter his most beautiful vessels, tapestries, and drinking utensils into the Sukkah.

✓ Pots, pans and plates are to be removed from the Sukkah after they are used being that they are repulsive, and it is belittling to the Sukkah. [The custom is not to enter pots into the Sukkah at all and rather the food is to be placed in a serving tray.]

✓ Belittling acts in the Sukkah: One may not do any belittling acts inside the Sukkah.

✓ The blessing of Leisheiv Basukkah: The blessing of 'Leisheiv Basukkah' is only said when eating a Kibeitza [55 grams] of Mezonos or Hamotzi [within Achilas Pras - 4 minutes]. It is not said prior to other actions of dwelling, such as a set drinking session, or spending time of leisure, or sleeping, in the Sukkah.

✓ Every time one eats a Kibeitza of Mezonos or Hamotzi in the Sukkah he is to say a blessing of Leisheiv Basukkah, if there was an interval of two hours between the previous time he ate and the current eating.

✓ The blessing of Leisheiv is recited after saying the blessing of the food, but prior to eating it.

✓ The Rebbe's custom is to look at Sechach upon saying Leisheiv.

✓ If one forgot to recite Leisheiv Basukkah prior to eating he is to say it upon remembering even if he has already finished eating.

✓ One must say the blessing of Leisheiv in every Sukkah that he eats a Kibeitza of Mezonos.

✓ If one enters into someone else's Sukkah in order to spend time of leisure, or in order to sleep in it, and he does not plan to eat a Kibeitza worth of Mezonos in that Sukkah, then he must say the blessing of Leisheiv Basukkah prior to relaxing, or sleeping, in it.

The Laws of Daled Minim

✓ Buy a set of Lulav and Esrog during Aseres Yimei Teshuvah. Some however write it is to be bought after Yom Kippur.

✓ Every person is to have his own set of Daled Minim.

✓ One is required to buy a set of Kosher Daled Minim on behalf of his [male] children.

✓ Owning on first day: On the 1st day of Sukkos [in Eretz Yisrael and the first two days of Sukkos in the Diaspora as will be explained next] one must use a set of Daled Minim which he personally owns. Therefore, when using someone else's Daled Minim one must receive it as a present on condition to return.

✓ Children: On the first day of Sukkos in Eretz Yisrael, and the first two days of Sukkos in the Diaspora, one is not to give his personal Daled Minim as a present on condition to return to any child below the age of 13 for a boy and 12 for a girl, to fulfill the Mitzvah.

✓ One may not buy any of the Daled Minim from a child under Bar Mitzvah, unless the child does not own the Daled Minim and is selling them on behalf of another person. If one already shook Daled Minim that was purchased from a Katan, then on the first day(s) one is to shake again without a blessing.

✓ Shaking in Jerusalem: Some Poskim rule that according to some Rishonim the shaking of Daled Minim in the old city of Jerusalem is a Biblical obligation for all seven days of the festival. Hence, when in the old city one is to use a set of Daled Minim that he owns, or receive it as a "Matana Al Menas Lehachzir". Likewise, the Daled Minim are to fulfill all the validation criteria required for the first day, such as Chasar and the like.

✓ Paying for the species after the holiday: One does not need to pay for the four species before Sukkos.

✓ How many of each species is one to take: One may not use for the Mitzvah more than 1 Esrog, 1 Lulav, and 2 Aravos. However, one may add onto the 3 Hadassim. One should try to add at least 3 more Hadassim to the minimal three required [for a total of six Hadassim].

✓ Water the Lulav, Hadassim and Aravos throughout the days of Sukkos.

✓ Replace the Hadassim and Aravos as the days go on, in accordance to need. One is not to stick the new Hadassim and Aravos into the knot which binds the Minim to the Lulav, as this causes leaves to shear and can invalidate the branch.

✓ On Yom Tov, don't carry Daled Minim in an area without an Eiruv if it does not serve a need.

✓ Throughout Sukkos one may not smell the Hadassim. One is to avoid smelling an Esrog even on Shabbos.

Binding the Lulav:
✓ Bind the Lulav on Erev Sukkos inside the Sukkah. [The Rebbe would do so after midday.]
✓ One is to personally bind the Lulav. Women and children are not to do so for a man's Lulav.
✓ The Chabad custom is not to use the Lulav pockets.
✓ One makes two knots on the Lulav itself using Lulav leaves. One then places a Hadas on the right, left and center of the Lulav, placing the Aravos in between in an inconspicuous fashion. The Hadassim should cover over the 2 knots on the Lulav. One then binds three knots onto the Hadassim and Aravos, all three should be within the space of 1 handbreadth (8 centimeters). It is proper to bind the Hadassim and Aravos towards the bottom of the Lulav in order to also hold on to them when doing the mitzvah. If one did not do so, he has nevertheless fulfilled the Mitzvah.
✓ The spine of the Lulav must reach at least one Tefach above the Hadassim/Aravos of the Lulav. The top of the spine is defined as the area where it begins to split into other leaves.

How to Bentch Lulav:
✓ Awaken early in the morning to perform the Mitzvah of Daled Minim.
✓ Do not eat before shaking the Lulav. If, however one will not be able to shake until after midday he should eat beforehand.
✓ Shake the Lulav inside the Sukkah.
✓ All the 4 Minim must be held top side up [the Esrog with its Pitam facing up].
✓ A right-handed person holds the Lulav in his right hand and the Esrog in his left hand, while a left-handed person holds the Lulav in his left hand and the Esrog in his right hand. The exact order of when the Lulav and Esrog are lifted will be explained next.
✓ The blessing process:
   1. One faces east [not specifically towards Jerusalem] throughout the blessing and shaking

process.

2. One takes hold of the Lulav in his right hand [if he's right-handed, as explained above].
3. The spine of the Lulav faces the person.
4. The Esrog remains on the table and is not lifted until after the blessing. One then says the Bracha of Al Netilas Lulav and lifts the Esrog in his left hand [if he is right-handed as explained above. A lefty lifts the Esrog in his right hand]. On the first day of Sukkos one now says [after lifting the Esrog] the blessing of Shehechiyanu.
5. One then adjoins the top third of the Esrog [thus having the Esrog in a slightly slanted position] with the Lulav/Hadassim and Aravos. Throughout the shaking, one remains holding the Lulav in his right hand and the Esrog in his left hand [for one who is right-handed].
6. One then shakes the Lulav with the adjoined Esrog three times in six different directions. One first shakes three times southeast [towards one's right], then three times northeast [towards one's left], then three times east [frontwards], three times up, three times down, and three times west.
7. When shaking towards west, the first two times one shakes to southwest [towards one's back on his right side] and then shakes it completely towards west.
8. Throughout the shaking, the Esrog remains covered by one's hand, until the last shake where one reveals the Esrog slightly.
9. The Lulav remains facing upwards throughout all of the shakings. It is not to be turned upside down when one shakes it downwards.
10. The Lulav is to be shaken after each Holacha [stretching away from the chest] prior to the Hovah [bringing back to the chest].

Kashrus of Lulav:
✓ Its spine is at least 32cm. and will extend a Tefach past Hadassim.
✓ Its Tiyomes is completely closed on its top.
✓ The Tiyomes is double leafed from top to bottom.
✓ The majority of the other leaves are also majority closed.
✓ The Tiyomes is not cut on its top.
✓ The Lulav is not bent to any side. The Lulav is straight.
✓ The leaves are not bent.
✓ The Tiyomes is not dry.
✓ Some prefer that the Lulav contain a Kara brown covering.

Kashrus of Esrog:
✓ Verify there are no missing pieces anywhere from the Esrog.
✓ Verify it does not have a broken Pitam.
✓ Verify it does not have a broken Oketz.
✓ Verify the Chotem is clean of a Chazazis or color change.
✓ Bletlach are Kosher.
✓ Verify that below the Chotem there is not two Chazazis, or two-color changes.
✓ Verify if it came from Israel that it has a Hashgacha.
✓ The color is to be completely yellow.

Kashrus of Hadassim:
- ✓ It is at least 24 cm. long.
- ✓ The first 24 cm from the top is completely Meshulash, or at the very least majority Meshulash.
- ✓ The top is not cut off.
- ✓ Remove random leaves.

Kashrus of Aravos:
- ✓ It is at least 24 cm.
- ✓ The first 24 cm from the top has all of its leaves, or at the very least majority.
- ✓ The top is not cut off.

Erev Sukkos:
- ✓ Increase in Tzedakah on Erev Sukkos.
- ✓ Bake Challahs for Yom Tov in the honor of Yom Tov.
- ✓ Cut the nails on Erev Sukkos in honor of Yom Tov.
- ✓ Get a haircut on Erev Sukkos.
- ✓ Prepare sweets for children in fulfilling Mitzvah of Simcha.
- ✓ Buy wife jewelry or clothing for Simcha.
- ✓ Do not eat a meal from the 10th hour of the day until the Yom Tov starts. This is approximately three hours before sunset. The above is only with regards to a set meal [i.e. 55 grams of bread] however it is permitted to eat a mere snack up until sunset and there is no need to refrain from doing so. If one transgressed or forgot and did not eat prior to the 10th hour, then on Erev Sukkos he may not eat a meal past the 10th hour.
- ✓ Bathe one's body in hot water on Erev Sukkos in honor of Yom Tov.
- ✓ Whenever Sukkos falls on Thursday one performs an Eiruv Tavshilin on Erev Sukkos [Wednesday] in the Diaspora.
- ✓ Bind the Lulav in the Sukkah. One should be meticulous to bind the Lulav himself as opposed to having someone else do it for him.
- ✓ Verifying the validity of the Sukkah: Before leaving to Shul for Mincha on Erev Sukkos, one is to verify the validity of the Sukkah and confirm that everything is in order.
- ✓ Candle lighting: One first lights the candles and then says the blessing of "Baruch Ata Hashem Elokeinu Melech Haolam Asher Kidishanu Bimitzvosav Vetzivanu Lehadlik Neir Shel Yom Tov". This blessing is then followed by the blessing of Shehechiyanu.
- ✓ Light the candles prior to sunset at the same time that they are lit on Erev Shabbos.
- ✓ The candles are to be lit within the Sukkah. If this is not possible [such as due to safety reasons] then one is to light inside.

The First day[s] of Yom Tov
- ✓ The Seder of Kiddush: Askinu, Hagafen, Asher Bachar Banu, Leisheiv, Shehechiyanu. The Rebbe's custom is to look at Sechach upon saying Leisheiv.
- ✓ Having in mind by Shehechiyanu: The Shehechiyanu is going on both the holiday and the Sukkah.
- ✓ Dip Challah in honey: It is customary of some to dip the Challah in honey throughout all the Yom Tov [and Shabbos] meals through Simchas Torah.
- ✓ Leisheiv Basukkah for the household: The household members who heard Kiddush are to say

the blessing of Leisheiv Basukkah after saying the blessing of Hamotzi.
- ✓ How much to eat: One must eat over a Kibeitza of bread in the Sukkah on 1st and 2nd night [in the Diaspora]. One should try to eat before midnight.
- ✓ Ushpizin: In addition to the company of Avraham, Yitzchak, Yaakov…. each night in ones Sukkah there is a tradition that the Chassidic Rabbeim also come to visit, starting with the Baal Shem Tov until the Rebbe Rashab. It is not our custom to say anything for the Ushpizin, however one should say a Dvar Torah mentioning the guest of that night.
- ✓ Yaaleh Veyavo in Bentching: If one forgot Yaaleh Veyavo in Birchas Hamazon then by the first two meals of Yom Tov one is to repeat Birchas Hamazon.
- ✓ Waking early for shaking Lulav: One is to awake early to fulfill the Mitzvah of Daled Minim especially on the first day of Sukkos.
- ✓ Simchas Beis Hashoeiva: Simchas Beis Hashoeiva begins on the 1st night of Sukkos.
- ✓ Hallel: The complete Hallel is recited throughout all 7 days of Sukkos and Shemini Atzeres. One holds on to Lulav during Hallel, and picks up also the Esrog only when it is needed to be shaken. We shake the Lulav a total of 4 times in Hallel. One who said a blessing on the Lulav before Hallel is only to shake the Lulav three times in Hallel, omitting the shaking in Ana Hashem.
- ✓ Hoshanos: Immediately after Hallel, prior to Kaddish, it is customary to circle the Bimah one time holding on to the Lulav and Esrog. One is to hold the Lulav and Esrog in two separate hands, the Lulav in his right hand and the Esrog in his left.
- ✓ One says the word Hoshana prior to each one of the words said for that day. Upon reaching the words upon which one begins to encircle, one is to say Hoshana prior and after each word. One places the Sefer Torah on the Bimah. One without a Lulav does not go around and rather holds on to the Sefer Torah.
- ✓ Day Kiddush: Say Leisheiv Basukkah after Hagafen.
- ✓ Havdalah: One says Havdalah in the Sukkah saying Leisheiv Basukkah. No candle or Besamim is used.

Chol Hamoed:
- ✓ One Davens a regular weekday Shemoneh Esrei for Maariv, Shacharis and Mincha, although adding Yaaleh Veyavo to the prayer. If one forgot to recite Yaaleh Veyavo in Shemoneh Esrei he must repeat the prayer.
- ✓ Throughout the eight/nine days of Sukkos and Shemini Atzeres, one is required to recite the complete Hallel with a blessing.
- ✓ It is a Biblical command for one to rejoice, himself, his wife, his children and his entire household, throughout all days of Yom Tov, including Chol Hamoed.
- ✓ A man is to drink a Revius of wine every day of Yom Tov, including Chol Hamoed.
- ✓ Initially, it is a Mitzvah for one to have a meal with bread twice on Chol Hamoed, once by day and once by night.]
- ✓ Recite the 6 Zechiros.
- ✓ Eat and drink delicacies and do other forms of Simcha.
- ✓ During Chol Hamoed, one recites Yaaleh Veyavo in Birchas Hamazon. If one forgot to recite it, he does not repeat Birchas Hamazon.
- ✓ It is customary amongst Jewry to perform a joyous gathering of song and dance throughout the nights of the festival of Sukkos, in commemoration of the Simchas Beis Hashoeiva which was experienced in Temple times on this Holiday.

✓ Many are accustomed to gather and visit Jerusalem during Sukkos, just as was done during Aliyah Laregel by Temple times.

Shabbos Chol Hamoed:
✓ Read Haftorah of Shabbos Chol Hamoed on Erev Shabbos.
✓ Hodu is omitted. Patach Eliyahu is recited.
✓ One begins the Maariv prayer from Mizmor Ledavid.
✓ In Lecha Dodi, the wording of Besimcha instead of Berina is recited.
✓ The following passages prior to Kiddush are read in an undertone: Shalom Aleichim, Eishes Chayil, Mizmor Ledavid Hashem Ro'i, Da hi Se'udasa.
✓ Hoshanos is not recited on Shabbos Chol Hamoed.

Hoshana Raba:
✓ Slightly increase in candles on Hoshana Raba just as is done on Yom Kippur.
✓ It is a custom of Jewry to remain awake throughout the entire night of Hoshana Raba.
✓ One reads the entire Sefer Devarim [prior to midnight], followed by reading the entire Sefer Tehillim [after midnight], and passages from the Zohar selected in the Tikkun.
✓ After the Tikkun, one eats an apple dipped in honey in the Sukkah. Prior to eating the apple dipped in honey one washes his hands the same way one washes for bread, but without a blessing.
✓ Those who are meticulous immerse in a Mikvah before dawn.
✓ Some Poskim rule that marital relations are to be avoided on the night of Hoshana Raba.
✓ One is to abstain from mundane activity until after leaving Shul [after Shacharis].
✓ It is proper to add in charity on Hoshana Raba in order to sweeten the Gevuros.
✓ The knots are removed from the top part of the Lulav [by the spine] prior to Hallel.
✓ One is to take a set of five Aravos and purchase a set of Hoshanos for each family member.
✓ The custom is to bind the Aravos together using Lulav leaves.
✓ After finishing all the Hakafos and reciting the additional prayer of Hoshanos over water, one hits the Aravos five times on the ground.
✓ One must be very careful to never join the Aravos to the Lulav anytime.
✓ The custom of the Chabad Rabbeim was to gently "whip" their sons with the Hoshana branches.
✓ In Eretz Yisrael, one reads Shnayim Mikra Viechad Targum on Hoshanah Raba.
✓ It is customary to hold a festive meal after the conclusion of the prayers.
✓ Customarily, one dips the bread in honey during the meal.
✓ The custom is to eat kreplach during the meal.
✓ One is to refrain from beginning a meal [of bread] past the 10th hour of the day.
✓ Mincha is the last time that Ledavid is said.

Shemini Atzeres and Simchas Torah
✓ The blessing of Shehechiyanu is recited during candle lighting of Shemini Atzeres and Simchas Torah.
✓ Time is very precious-Dance!
✓ Seder at night: Regular Yom Tov Maariv is followed by Kaddish Shaleim and then Farbrengen. Then Ata Hareisa is recited three times, which is followed by Hakafos, and then Aleinu.

✓ <u>Does one still eat in the Sukkah?</u> On Shemini Atzeres outside Eretz Yisrael one eats and drinks in the Sukkah but without a Blessing. In Eretz Yisrael: One does not eat in the Sukkah.

✓ <u>Kiddush:</u> On the night of Simchas Torah it is customary for all men to say Kiddush on their own.

✓ Drink wine by meal.

✓ On Shemini Atzeres and Simchas Torah one does not dip the bread of Hamotzi in honey.

✓ <u>Hakafos:</u> One dances Hakafos on both nights with extreme joy. The Rebbe Rashab said that one draws down abundance of physical and spiritual blessing through the joy of dancing by Hakafos.

✓ One should increase the amount of lights in the Shul in honor of the Sifrei Torah that are removed.

✓ During the recital of Kerias Shema Al Hamita on the night of Simchas Torah, one is to make a resolution to spread Torah with Mesirus Nefesh.

✓ Marital relations are initially avoided on Simchas Torah.

✓ Hakafos is not done on Shemini Atzeres day.

✓ Yizkor is said on Shemini Atzeres.

✓ Announce Mashiv Haruach before Musaf of Shemini Atzeres. However, Morid Hatal is only said from the 7th of Cheshvan in Israel, and from the 6th December in Diaspora.

✓ On the eve of Simchas Torah [i.e. Shemini Atzeres in the Diaspora; Hoshana Raba in Eretz Yisrael] one is to read the Parsha of Vezos Habracha, Shnayim Mikra V'echad Targum.

✓ With the approach of sunset on the afternoon of Shemini Atzeres one enters the Sukkah (and eats or drinks something there) to bid it farewell.

✓ One may not prepare on the 1st day of Yom Tov on behalf of the 2nd day.

✓ On Simchas Torah, one does not eat or sleep in the Sukkah.

✓ <u>The Simchas Torah day Davening</u>: Kaddish Shaleim after Hallel, followed by Kiddush, followed by Ata Hareisa and Hakafos. After the conclusion of Hakafos, Ata Hareisa for Kerias Hatorah is recited, as well as Vayehi Binsoa and the thirteen Middos. Nesias Kapayim is only done by Shacharis. It is done with the same Niggun usually done by Musaf.

✓ <u>The day Hakafos:</u> During the day of Simchas Torah, the custom is to only perform 3.5 circles around the Bima as opposed to seven. Nevertheless, all seven liturgies of Hakafos is read. Thus, one reads a single Hakafa for every half circle of the Bimah, for a total of seven half circles corresponding to the reading of the seven Hakafos. All 3.5 circles of Hakafos are performed consecutively without dancing in between or placing Sefer Torah back in Aron or even announcing "Ad Kan Hakafa…". After the conclusion of the 3.5 circles the congregation dances. At the conclusion, the Sefer Torah is returned to the Aron without saying anything.

✓ It is customary for each man to get an Aliyah on Simchas Torah.

✓ For Kol Hanearim one person is to say a blessing on behalf of all the children. We do not spread a Tallis over the children.

Shaar Hachassidus-Chassidic insights on Sukkos

1. The Holiday:

- The commemoration: The holiday of Sukkos commemorates the miracles and wonders that were performed for the Jewish people while in the desert, and during the exodus. The Holiday is also considered a sequel to the High Holidays of Rosh Hashanah and Yom Kippur, as explained next.

- Draws down the light of the High Holidays: During the High Holidays, we draw down revelations of G-dliness for the coming year. This is likewise drawn down during the festival of Sukkos. The only difference is in regarding the method. That which was drawn down during the High Holidays in a mode of awe and reverence is drawn down again on Sukkos, with joy and exuberance. This particularly applies during Shemini Atzeres. Sukkos is a time of revelation of Or Ein Sof of Yom Kippur into the heart. It is however only in a way of Makif and hence is hinted to in the Sechach of the Sukkah which is also a Makif. On Shemini Atzeres however it is drawn down internally.

- An embrace from Hashem: Sukkos is the holiday which reveals the inner love experienced on Rosh Hashana. The Sukkah is like an embrace from Hashem. The verse of Min Hameitzar applies on Rosh Hashana while the verse of Merchav Kah applies during Sukkos. That is why the Simcha of Sukkos is done with water, the Nisuch Hamayim, as the Simcha is form such a high source that it can penetrate even water which does not have Simcha in it of itself.

2. The Sukkah

- The Hundred blows of Rosh Hashanah and the Sechach: On Rosh Hashanah, we blow the Shofar for a total of one hundred times. We blow 60 Tekios, 20 Teruos, and 20 Shevarim. This represents the exact Gematria of the word Sechach, which is 60-20-20. This Gematria emphasizes the previous point mentioned, that on Sukkos we draw down the same revelations of Rosh Hashanah.

- The cloud of the Yom Kippur Ketores and the Sechach: The Sechach represents the clouds of glory which escorted the Jewish people in the desert. It is also reminiscent of the cloud of incense that was offered in the Temple on the day of Yom Kippur.

- The Chassidic meaning behind the requirement of majority shade: The Sukkah represents the drawing of an Or Makif down below, to the Jew dwelling inside. Now, an Oar Makif is a very high level of G-dliness [level of Yashis Choshech Sisro] which can only be transmitted in a concealed fashion, hence the requirement for the Sukkah to retain majority shade.

- The Chassidic meaning behind allowing the stars to be seen: The Sukkah represents the drawing of an Or Makif down below to the Jew dwelling inside. The purpose of this Oar Makif is to be drawn internally into the Jew. This is represented by the stars which represent a glimmer of the Makif light.

- All our actions connect with Hashem: One of the lessons of the Sukkah is that every action a Jew performs is to be connected with Hashem. Just as the mundane actions performed in the Sukkah, is considered a Mitzvah, so too throughout the year, one can connect his mundane actions to Hashem, through performing them for the sake of Heaven.

3. The Daled Minim

- A Mitzvah of Unity: In general, the Mitzvah of the four species represents unity of the Jewish people, which is apparent in each of the four species as will be explained later on. This unity arouses the unity of the Divine Sefirot of G-D above in the world of Atzilus. Amongst the Sefirot there are opposing attributes, such as the attribute of kindness and of severity. In order to effect unity amongst these attributes there is required to bring down to their level a very high revelation of G-dliness which to that level both the attributes of severity and of kindness will be nullified to, and thus allow for their unification. It is this level of G-dliness which the four species arouse above to be drawn down to the world of Atzilus and thus cause the unity. Further on will be explained how physically each one of the four species contains aspects of unity in them.

- Represents unity of the Jewish people: The aspect of unity is also apparent in the general unity of the four species being taken together. The Midrash explains how each one of the four species represents a different segment of Jewry, and how their being bound together represents their unity.

- Each species itself contains unity: Each of the four species contain a certain aspect of unity which differs from all other species in the world. Thus, there is a double aspect of unity in the four species. The unity found in each particular species, and the unity found by bringing the four species together, as explained above.

- The unity within the Lulav: The Lulav contain a certain aspect of unity which differs from all other branches in the world. All trees have their branches grow in various directions from their stem and do not follow any pattern of growth. A regular tree whose leaves have fallen, appears like a stem with many arms, each going in its own direction, thus leaving areas on the stem's branch bare. The date palm tree, however, has its branches grow in a set pattern, each branch growing from directly on top of the branch below it. Altogether, it forms a united pattern of branches which covers all of the spine of the palm branch. It is a branch from this tree that G-D commanded us to take to use for the Mitzvah of the four species- the Mitzvah of Unity.

- The representation of the Lulav within Jewry: The Midrash explains that the Lulav represents the Torah scholars who spend the majority of their time learning Torah. The connection between the two is that Torah is referred to as something of good taste. This corresponds to the taste of the dates which derive from the palm tree of which the Lulav is taken from.

- The unity of the Esrog: The unity within the Esrog: The Esrog contains a certain aspect of unity which differs from all other fruits in the world. All fruits have a season of growth during the year, while the Esrog remains on the tree for the entire year, throughout all four seasons. Thus, the Esrog fruit unifies all the seasons of the year.

- The representation of the Esrog within Jewry: The Midrash explains that the Esrog represents the people who spend their time performing Mitzvos and Gemilus Chassadim as well as learning Torah. Torah and Mitzvos correspond to the good taste and good smell found in the Esrog.

- The unity of the Hadas: The Hadas is only valid if it contains a majority of three leave sets that grow on the same line. This is unlike other leaves of a branch, in which the leaves grow in a scattered method, along the branch. This pattern followed by the leaves of the Hadas is the aspect of unity found in this branch, over that of other branches.

- The representation of the Hadas within Jewry: The Midrash explains that the Hadas represents the people who spend their time performing Mitzvos and Gemilus Chassadim, but not learning Torah. Mitzvos correspond to the good smell found in the Hadas.

- <u>The Meaning of the Aravah</u>: The Aravah is a big bushy tree that has its branches and leaves grow very close to each other. This represents brotherhood and was thus chosen for the Mitzvah of unity.
- <u>The representation of the Aravah within Jewry</u>: The Midrash explains that the Aravah represents the people who do not contain either Mitzvos or good deeds, as the Aravah contains neither a good taste nor smell. On the Holiday of Sukkos, all Jews unify together, including such Jews. The Baal Shem tov explains that the Aravah represents the simple Jew, who serves Hashem with utter simplicity.

Chapter 1: The Sukkah

1. Building the Sukkah:

A. The Mitzvah of building a Sukkah:

- The reason G-d commanded us to sit in a Sukkah for shade, is so we recall the miracles and wonders done for us in the desert, in which the clouds of glory surrounded us for shade, as protection from the sun. When dwelling in a Sukkah one must have intent to do so in order to fulfill G-d's command to sit in a Sukkah in commemoration of the Exodus. This obligation to have intent during the dwelling is learned from the verse "So you shall know".
- Must one have this intent every time he dwells in the Sukkah? Yes. Each time one eats in the Sukkah, and fulfills the Mitzvah of dwelling in the Sukkah, he is to intend to fulfill the Mitzvah for the above-mentioned reason of commemorating the exodus.
- Is everyone to have their own Sukkah? It is proper for each family to build their own Sukkah just like each person has his own house.
- Is a Shul required to build a Sukkah? It is accustomed to build a Sukkah in Shul for the sake of guests.

B. When to build the Sukkah:

- On Motzei Yom Kippur one begins building the Sukkah, [or at least talking about building it], in order to leave one Mitzvah and enter to another Mitzvah. It is a Mitzvah to build the entire Sukkah immediately the day after Yom Kippur, after one leaves Shul after Shacharis.
- May one build his Sukkah on Erev Sukkos? Ideally one is to complete the building of his Sukkah prior to 2.5 hours before sunset. If, however, it is past 2.5 hours before sunset and one has still not built his Sukkah, it may nevertheless still be built.
- Building a Sukkah on Chol Hamoed: One who did not build a Sukkah before the Holiday is to build his Sukkah on Chol Hamoed and dwell in it. This applies whether one did not build his Sukkah due to negligence or due to no fault of his own. This applies even at the end of the seventh day of Sukkos, nevertheless he is obligated to build a Sukkah in order to dwell in the Sukkah for the remaining moments.

C. Who may build the Sukkah:

- Should one personally build the Sukkah versus having someone else do so for him? It is proper for one to personally place the Sechach onto the Sukkah [and help build the walls] rather than have another person do so for him. [The Rabbeim were not particular to personally build their Sukkah, although it is recalled that the Rebbe was particular to always place some Sechach onto his Sukkah. It is told that Reb Hillel Paritcher was particular to help build the walls of the Sukkah. The Noam Elimelech explains that one is to personally toil to build the Sukkah in order to sanctify his limbs.]
- May women or children build the Sukkah? **Walls**: Women and children may help build the walls of the Sukkah, even initially. **Sechach**: Some Poskim rule that women and children are not initially to place the Sechach on the Sukkah. This applies even if an adult male Jew supervises them during the placing of the Sechach and tells them do it for the sake of the Mitzvah. Practically, it is best to initially be stringent like this opinion. However, in the event that a woman or child placed the Sechach on the Sukkah, the Sukkah is deemed valid and a blessing may be recited over it.
- May a gentile build the Sukkah? **Walls**: A gentile may help build the walls of the Sukkah. However, some write that a gentile should not build even the walls of the Sukkah. **Sechach:**

A gentile is not to initially place the Sechach on the Sukkah. If he already did so, the Sukkah is Kosher.

D. Ownership of the Sukkah:
* <u>Must one dwell in the same Sukkah throughout Sukkos?</u> One is not required to dwell within the same Sukkah throughout the seven days of Sukkos and he can thus leave his Sukkah and dwell in another person's Sukkah.
* <u>A borrowed Sukkah:</u> One fulfills his obligation with a borrowed Sukkah.
* <u>A Sukkah with joint ownership:</u> One fulfills his obligation with a jointly owned Sukkah, and he is not required to request permission from the other owner to dwell in it.
* <u>A stolen Sukkah:</u> One who seized another's property which contains a Sukkah: If one forcibly removed the owner from his Sukkah and stole it and dwelled in it, he fulfills his obligation.
* <u>May one say a blessing in such a Sukkah:</u> If one transgressed and hijacked someone's Sukkah, although he fulfills his obligation nevertheless, he may not say a blessing 'Leisheiv Basukkah.'
* <u>May one enter someone else's Sukkah without permission?</u> One may not initially enter another person's Sukkah without permission even if he does not intend to steal it from him, if the person is currently in his Sukkah. However, it is permitted to enter his Sukkah even initially while he is not there.

E. Where is the Sukkah to be built
* <u>May one build a Sukkah in someone else's property without permission?</u> One may not build a Sukkah in someone else's property.
* <u>May one build a Sukkah in a public property?</u> Initially one may not build a Sukkah in a public area such as on a city street or sidewalk and the like of places that people pass by. This applies even if the entire city is of Jewish population and certainly the Jews do not mind one building his Sukkah there. One is to protest against anyone who makes a Sukkah in a public area. Nevertheless, Bedieved if one built a Sukkah in a public property, he fulfills his obligation. If one transgressed and built a Sukkah in a public property although he fulfills his obligation, nevertheless he may not say a blessing of 'Leisheiv Basukkah'. [However, many Poskim rule one may even initially build a Sukkah in a public property and say a blessing, and so is the custom. This especially applies if one has received permission from the city municipality.]
* If one does not have a permit to build in his property may one build a Sukkah there? Yes.
* If the city municipality gave permission for one to build his Sukkah in public property may one do so? Yes.
* May one build his Sukkah on his sidewalk? Only with permission of the municipality.
* May one build a Sukkah in the joint property of an apartment complex, such as in the parking lot, or garden/courtyard? One may only do so if he receives permission from the building management and/or the occupants of the building. This applies even if one owns an apartment or lives in the complex.
* <u>Is a mobile Sukkah valid?</u> A Sukkah that is attached to the back of a pick-up truck is valid so long as a normal wind cannot blow off the walls or the Sechach. Such a Sukkah is valid even when the car is moving and even if it does not have a floor attached to it.

- <u>May one make a Sukkah on a tree?</u> Yes. However, he cannot climb it on Shabbos or Yom Tov.
- <u>Building Sukkah over a lawn</u>: It is forbidden to pour liquid over grass, plants, [trees] and the like on Shabbos or Yom Tov. Due to this reason, when eating outside over a lawn which contains grass, plants or trees one must beware not to spill or pour water over it. [Hence, one should not build his Sukkah over a lawn, as it is very difficult to avoid any spillage. If necessary, one should cover the lawn with a makeshift floor.]

F. The dimensions of the Sukkah:
- <u>The height:</u> The Sukkah must be more than 10 Tefachim high, and may not be more than 20 Amos [10 meters] high. This means that the Sechach may not be a height of 20 Amos from the floor of the Sukkah.
- <u>The length/width:</u> A Sukkah must have the minimum size of seven by seven Tefachim [56 x 56 cm.]. If it does not have this minimum size, it is invalid. There is no maximum size for the Sukkah. [The Sukkah must be at least seven Tefachim both in width and length. If it is less than seven Tefachim in either length of width, then even if it contains a total space of 7 square Tefach, it is invalid. For example, a Sukkah that is 20 Tefach by 6 Tefach is invalid.]
- <u>Corner areas and rooms in a Sukkah:</u> A Sukkah that contains a corner area that is less than 7x7 Tefachim is invalid, and does not join the rest of the Sukkah. [Likewise, rooms that are separated with Mechitzos are invalid if they contain a dimension that is less than 7x7 Tefachim. Thus, not only must the entire Sukkah be 7x7 Tefachim, but any area of the Sukkah that is separate from the other areas must also contain a dimension of 7x7 Tefachim.]
- <u>May one put up a Mechitza between men and women in a Sukkah?</u> A Mechitza may only be set up in a Sukkah if it leaves a dimension of 7x7 Tefachim on each side of the Mechitza, otherwise that area that contains less than 7x7 Tefachim becomes invalidated.
- <u>Does a Sukkah require a Mezuzah?</u> A Sukkah is not obligated to have a Mezuzah.

G. The laws of the walls
- <u>How many walls does a Sukkah require?</u> It is a Mitzvah Min Hamuvchar to have a four walled Sukkah and so is the custom. Likewise, it is customary to make complete walls rather than walls that contain breaches. If one is unable to make four complete walls then it is better to make three complete walls and have one side be open without a wall than to make four walls with breaches. Nevertheless, from the letter of the law it suffices to have two full walls with a third wall using the rule of Lavud. This means that one is not required to have a full third wall but rather can have a partial wall, and following the rules of Lavud, it is considered a full third wall. The exact details of how this is accomplished will be explained below.
- According to the custom, one is to make four complete walls without resorting to the rule of Lavud. However, from the letter of the law it suffices even if all four walls are built using Lavud.
- <u>The criteria for a valid wall?</u> A wall is only considered a valid wall if the following four conditions are fulfilled:
  1) <u>Does not move with wind:</u> A wall is only defined as a wall if it is unable to move with a common wind. If a common wind can blow the wall, as is the case with sheet walls, then it is invalid. [Some Poskim limit this only to a case that a common wind can move the wall a three Tefach distance forward or upward.]

2) <u>Is height of 10 Tefach</u>: A wall is only defined as a wall if its height reaches ten Tefach [80 cm] from the ground. If the wall's height reaches below ten Tefach from the ground it is invalid. If the wall reaches ten Tefach from the ground but is elevated from the ground, then if it is within three Tefach from the ground and reaches to ten Tefach from the ground, it is valid. Thus, technically, one can have a wall which is 7.1 Tefach tall and place it 2.9 Tefach from the ground and it is valid.

3) <u>Is within three Tefach from ground</u>: The wall must be within three Tefach from the ground. Even if the wall is very high, if it is not placed within three Tefach from the ground, it is invalid.

4) <u>Is within three Tefach from Sechach</u>: The wall must be within three [**horizontal**] Tefach of the Sechach for it to be validated as a wall for that Sechach. [This however only applies if there is empty space between the wall and the Sechach. If, however, there is invalid Sechach in the above area, then the wall remains valid so long as it is within 4 Amos [196 cm] of the Sechach.

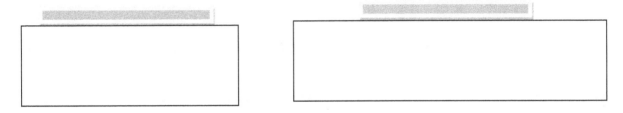

- <u>How many walls must fulfill these conditions</u>: At least two of the Sukkah walls must meet the above requirements while a third wall is to meet the requirements of Lavud. Any wall that does not meet the above requirements, is invalid.

- <u>May one use as one of the three Halachically required walls a sliding or removable door?</u> If at the initial time that the Sukkah was erected, the walls were valid, and the doors were closed, then it is permitted later on to open and close this door, even though it nullifies the Sukkah at the time of its opening. One must note that on Shabbos and Yom Tov it would remain forbidden to open and close this door, being it invalidates, and then validates the Sukkah when opened and then closed.

- <u>How long must each wall be?</u> The minimum size of a Sukkah is seven by seven Tefachim [56 x 56 cm]. Thus, technically one is required to have three walls which are seven Tefach long. However, using the Biblical rules of Lavud, it suffices to have one wall of 7 Tefach. This can be accomplished in the following way: One has a single wall which is seven Tefach long, with another wall of 4 Tefach horizontal to it, within 3 Tefach from the end of the 7 Tefach wall. The third wall can then be made with Lavud and Tzuras Hapesach. Thus, it is possible to make a Sukkah with only one wall of seven Tefach. Nevertheless, as stated above, the custom is to make complete walls without resorting to the rules of Lavud.

- <u>How does one make a third wall using Lavud?</u> If one has two walls which are parallel to each other then one is to place a Mechitza which is 4 Tefach wide [32cm.] within three Tefach [24cm.] from the end of one of the walls. Hence, using Lavud one has a total of 7 Tefach.

2.9 T

- <u>Sechach that extends past the walls of a Sukkah:</u> If a Sukkah contains Sechach that extends past the back wall of the Sukkah, and the two horizontal walls likewise extend past the back wall [Figure A], then if that area is at least 7x 7 Tefachim, it is Kosher so long as it provides majority shade. If a Sukkah contains three walls and there is Sechach extending past the open side and one of the walls of the Sukkah extends together with the Sechach [Figure B], then if that area is 7x7, that area is considered part of the Sukkah and it is permitted to eat under it even though it contains only one extending wall.

Figure A

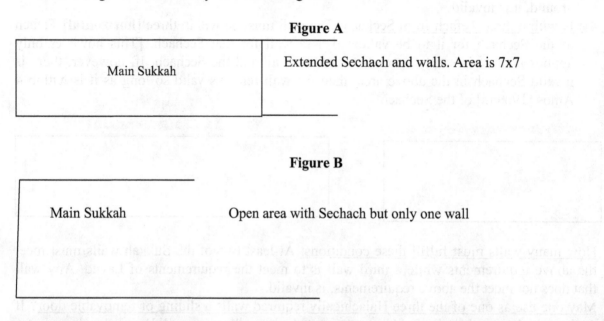

| Main Sukkah | Extended Sechach and walls. Area is 7x7 |

Figure B

| Main Sukkah | Open area with Sechach but only one wall |

- <u>The material of the walls:</u> The walls may be made using any material [that does not move with a common wind], even if the material does not lend shade to the Sukkah [such as glass or transparent plastic]. Nevertheless, one is not to use materials that give off a foul odor or which dry out within 7 days. The walls may be made even initially from material that is Halachically unfit for use as Sechach.
- <u>Using sheets as a wall:</u> One is not to use sheets whether of material or plastic as a wall being that it is difficult to ascertain that the sheets will not move with the wind. However, it is permitted to use sheets if one places poles within three Tefach using Lavud to make the wall, as in such a case even if the sheets move with the wind the wall remains Kosher due to the poles which are Lavud. [According to all, Bedieved if one used sheet walls that do not move with the wind the Sukkah is Kosher even if Lavud was not used.]
- <u>Practically are Sukkos with plastic walls initially valid?</u> If the walls allow the placing of string or poles to perform Lavud to make three walls then it is valid according to all even initially. However, if Lavud is not being used one should not use such a Sukkah being it is possible that the walls will become loose and move with the wind. However, from the letter of the law if the plastic does not move with the wind it is valid. Some Poskim rule that it is even initially permitted to use plastic sheets if they are tightly attached as it is not possible to be with the wind.
- <u>Writing verses on the wall of one's Sukkah:</u> One may not write or engrave versus on items or walls of the Sukkah as it is forbidden to write verses of the Torah unless one is writing them

in a complete Sefer, and engraving is just like writing regarding this matter. [Practically, many are lenient in this matter, especially if one is skipping a few letters from the verse.]

H. The order of building-Setting up the walls before the Sechach?

- One is not to place the Sechach over the [frame of the] Sukkah prior to building the [Halachically valid] walls.
- If one transgressed and first placed the Sechach over the frame and only then built the walls, some Poskim rule the Sukkah is valid. Other Poskim, however, rule the Sukkah is invalid. [Practically, we rule that the Sukkah is invalid, and one is hence to undo the Sechach and replace it. It suffices to simply lift the entire Sechach one Tefach and then replace it.]
- If after building the Sukkah in its proper order, the walls blew off, must one remove the Sechach prior to replacing the walls? In a case that the Sukkah was erected in the correct order [first walls and then Sechach] then it is not necessary to remove the Sechach prior to fixing the walls, if the walls fell over. However, some Poskim rule that if this occurred before Sukkos one is required to replace the Sechach.
- May one use as one of the three Halachically required walls a sliding or removable door? Using a door that will be opened and closed as one of the three Halachically required walls enters into the above question of causing the Sechach to hover over the Sukkah at a time that the Sukkah is invalid due to the opened door. Practically, as stated above, if at the initial time that the Sukkah was erected, the walls were valid, and the doors were closed, then it is permitted later on to open and close this door, even though it nullifies the Sukkah at the time of its opening. However, according to the stringent approach brought in the previous Q&A, one is to avoid opening the door before the start of Sukkos, and if one does so, is to replace the Sechach. One must note that on Shabbos and Yom Tov it would remain forbidden to open and close this door, being it invalidates, and then validates the Sukkah when opened and then closed.

I. The Sukkah furniture:

- May one eat in a Sukkah with the table outside? No. One who does so does not fulfill his obligation. Some Poskim require at least a Tefach of the table to be inside the Sukkah in which case it is valid. Others require that majority of the table to be inside the Sukkah.

J. An old Sukkah-Using a Sukkah that remains intact throughout the year:

- The Sukkah must be made only in order to give shade: Just as the clouds of glory were there to give us shade from the sun, similarly the Sukkah is only valid when made in order to only give shade. If it was made to serve for also other purposes, such as storage and the like then it is not considered a Sukkah but rather a house and is inherently invalid.
- Retractable roof: If the Sukkah [with its Sechach] is used throughout the year as one's dwelling place of eating and sleeping and performance of majority of one's actions, it is invalid, and [all] the Sechach must be lifted and placed back on each year before Sukkos. It suffices to simply lift up [all] the Sechach and place it back down. [It does not suffice to simply lift a Tefach worth of Sechach.] If, however, one does not live in the Sukkah, even if he uses it for certain purposes, then it remains valid, [and follows the law to be explained]. [Thus, a Sukkah that is built in one's house under a retractable roof and left intact the entire year, since one lives in this Sukkah throughout the year, he is required to renew the Sechach each year before Sukkos.]

- <u>An old Sukkah</u> A Sukkah which was built for the purpose of fulfilling the Mitzvah is valid even if it was built towards the beginning of the year. [Thus, if one never took down the previous year's Sukkah, it may be used for the current Sukkos holiday without needing any modification.] If the Sukkah was built for the sake of shade, then if this was done within thirty days before Sukkos, it is valid. If it was made prior to 30 days before Sukkos, one must renew something in the Sukkah for the sake of the Mitzvah. The definition of a renewed action is to place new Sechach at least the size of 1x1 Tefach for the sake of the Mitzvah, or to place Sechach from one end of the Sukkah to another even if it is less than one Tefach. Regarding the walls, even if they were made from the beginning of the year for shade, one does not need to renew anything for it to be valid and renewing the Sechach suffices.
- <u>If one did not take down the Sukkah from the previous year, and it is not used as a dwelling area, does it require an action of renewal to be performed to its Sechach?</u> Some Poskim rule the Sukkah is only valid without renewal if it was made for the sake of the Mitzvah after the passing of the previous Sukkos. If, however, it was made before the previous Sukkos then an act of renewal is required prior to the coming Sukkos, as explained above regarding a Sukkah made for shade prior to 30 days. Other Poskim however rule the Sukkah remains valid and does not require any modification. It is implied from Admur like this latter opinion.
- <u>If one's Sukkah [with its Sechach] serves as a pergola throughout the year, does its Sechach require renewal?</u> Some Poskim rule one is not required to do any action of renewal in such a case.
- <u>If one's Sukkah serves as part of one's home, must all the Sechach be lifted and replaced each year before Sukkos?</u> Example: One has a retractable roof in one of the rooms of his house which serves as a Sukkah during the Holiday. May one leave the Sechach remaining throughout the year and simply open the roof to use the Sukkah, or does the Sechach require removal and replacement? If one uses the room for living purposes, then all the Sechach must be lifted and then replaced before Sukkos. This applies even if one has a retractable roof over the Sechach, nevertheless it does not suffice to simply open the roof. If, however, one does not live in this room, then it suffices to simply open the roof before Sukkos. Some Poskim however side that even if one lives in the room, it suffices to open the retractable roof.
- <u>The definition of living:</u> Seemingly, it is only defined that one is living in the room regarding the above law, if one uses the room for eating, sleeping and all one's regular house activity. If, however, one does not eat or sleep in the room then it is not considered a living area and hence does not require removal of all the Sechach prior to Sukkos.

K. Benefiting from the Sukkah
- <u>Using the Sechach of the Sukkah for other purposes:</u> The Sechach of the Sukkah is considered like Hekdesh. Hence it is Biblically forbidden to use it throughout the seven days of Sukkos. This applies to all the Sechach in the Sukkah, even if the Sukkah is much larger than its minimum requirement of 7x7. This applies even if the Sechach fell off the Sukkah, or the Sukkah became destroyed and hence its Mitzvah became nullified, nevertheless, it is Biblically forbidden to use the Sechach throughout the days of Sukkos.
- <u>May one make a stipulation on the Sechach?</u> No.
- <u>May one get benefit from the walls of the Sukkah?</u> Rabbinically it is forbidden to use the walls throughout the seven days of Sukkos. This applies even if the Sukkah fell. This applies to all four walls of the Sukkah. If, however, one designated which wall is the fourth wall that

is only being erected as a Mitzvah Min Hamuvchar then that wall may be benefited from. Likewise, if one first built three walls and then built a fourth wall, that fourth wall is valid.

- What form of benefit is permitted: It is only forbidden to remove the Sechach or walls and then use it, however one may use it while it is in its erect state such as to place items on it or smell it if it contains Besamim.
- May one make a stipulation on the walls? No. It does not help to make a stipulation before Sukkos to be able to use the walls during Sukkos.
- May one lean on the walls? Yes.
- May one use a fridge or closet that is used as a wall for the Sukkah? Yes.
- May one benefit and use the floor of the Sukkah? Some Poskim rule that one may not benefit from the floor of the Sukkah if the floor was built for the Sukkah. Thus, if one placed a rug in his Sukkah he may not use them during Sukkos. However, the ground may be benefited from.
- From when does the benefit prohibition take effect? The prohibition takes affect from the first time one dwells in the Sukkah, beginning from the night of the 15th. However, prior to dwelling in it for the first time, it does not become holy. This applies whether or not the Sukkah was built for the sake of the Mitzvah or for the sake of shade, nevertheless it does not receive holiness until he dwells in it. Thus, one may use and benefit from this Sechach and walls and decorations.

L. The decorations of a Sukkah:
- It is a widespread, old age, custom amongst Jewry to decorate the Sukkah with different ornaments and valuables. The Chabad Custom, however, is not to decorate the Sukkah.
- Benefiting from, or removing, the Sukkah decorations: All decorations of a Sukkah are forbidden in benefit just like the Sukkah itself, throughout the entire holiday of Sukkos. This applies even if the decoration fell on Sukkos. Thus, if one placed grapes or other fruits as a decoration he may not eat them during Sukkos. However, if one stipulates before Sukkos, before Bein Hashmashos, that he reserves the right to use them during Bein Hashmashos of all the days it is not forbidden in benefit. Practically, today the custom is to allow removing the ornaments on Shabbos and Yom Tov and one is allowed to use them even if one did not stipulate beforehand being that the custom has become to allow doing so and it is hence considered as if one stipulated. Nevertheless, initially it is proper to stipulate on this matter from before Yom Tov.
- From when does the benefit prohibition take effect? The prohibition takes affect from the first time one dwells in the Sukkah, beginning from the night of the 15th. However, prior to dwelling in it for the first time it does not become holy. This applies whether or not the Sukkah was built for the sake of the Mitzvah or for the sake of shade nevertheless it does not receive holiness until he dwells in it. Thus, one may use and benefit from this Sechach and walls and decorations.
- Are the Sukkah decorations Muktzah on Shabbos/Yom Tov? Ideally, if a stipulation was not made, then the decorations are Muktzah on Shabbos/Yom Tov. However, in light of the above custom to move the items even without stipulation, the decorations are not Muktzah even if a stipulation was not made.
- Are pictures placed in a Sukkah considered Noy Sukkah and Muktzah on Shabbos/Yom Tov? Pictures are considered "Noy Sukkah" and hence should not initially be removed from the Sukkah unless one stipulated beforehand, as explained above. Nevertheless, in light of the

above custom to move the items even without stipulation, one may in a time of need move the pictures from the Sukkah even if a stipulation was not made. Accordingly, the pictures are not considered Muktzah on Shabbos and Yom Tov, and may be replaced if they fell [although seemingly it is best to do so using a Shinuiy if a stipulation was not explicitly made].

M. Taking apart the Sukkah:

- Using the Sechach of the Sukkah for other purposes: The Sechach of the Sukkah is considered like Hekdesh. Hence it is Biblically forbidden to use it throughout the seven days of Sukkos. This applies to all the Sechach in the Sukkah, even if the Sukkah is much larger than its minimum requirement of 7x7. This applies even if the Sechach fell off the Sukkah or the Sukkah became destroyed and hence its Mitzvah became nullified nevertheless it is Biblically forbidden to use the Sechach throughout the days of Sukkos.

- What is one to do with the Sukkah after Sukkos? After Sukkos one is not required to bury the wood used for Sechach and it may be used and benefited from as one sees fit. Nevertheless, it is proper to beware not to use it for a belittling use as this is disrespectful to the Mitzvah. It goes without saying that one may not trample on the Sechach in order not to do a belittling act with it.

- Taking apart a Sukkah during Chol Hamoed: One may not take apart his Sukkah [during Chol Hamoed, even] on the seventh day. [Some Poskim rule that this applies even if one no longer needs to use the Sukkah, such as if he has another Sukkah available. Other Poskim however are lenient in this matter in a time of need.]

- May one take apart his Sukkah during Chol Hamoed if he plans to rebuild it elsewhere? Some Poskim rule it is forbidden to take apart a Sukkah during Chol Hamoed even if one desires to erect it in a different area as by doing so one is nullifying its holiness. Other Poskim rule it is permitted if one plans to rebuild the Sukkah in another area.

- What is one to do regarding a portable fold up Sukkah? It is best to erect the Sukkah on Chol Hamoed and it is then permitted to undo the Sukkah according to ones needs.

2. The laws of the Sechach:
A. The intended use of the Sechach:
- <u>For shade:</u> Just as the clouds of glory were there to give us shade from the sun, similarly the Sukkah is only valid when made in order to only give shade. If it was made to serve for also other purposes, such as storage and the like then it is not considered a Sukkah but rather a house and is inherently invalid.
- <u>Must the Sechach be placed for the sake of the Mitzvah?</u> It is not necessary for the Sechach to be placed on the Sukkah for the sake of the Mitzvah, so long as it is placed for the sake of shade. Thus, even if those included in the Roshei Teivos [initials] of Ganbach-Rakvash made a Sukkah for the sake of shade and not for the sake of the Mitzvah, the Sukkah remains valid. [Nevertheless, Lechatchila, one is not to have a person listed in Ganbach-Rakvash place the Sechach on the Sukkah, as explained above regarding women and children.]
- The word Ganbach stands for the following people: Goyim/Gentiles; Women; Animals; Kuti
- The word Rakvash stands for the following: Roim/Shepherd's; Kayatzim [Guard of produce piled within a field for drying purposes.]; Barganim [Guards of a city]; Shomreiy Hasadah [guards of a field]

B. Minimum amount of Sechach-How much Sechach shade must the Sukkah contain:
- The Sechach must provide enough shade for there to be more shade than sunlight in the Sukkah. Thus, even if the Sechach is very thin and thus allows sunlight to enter, so long as it provides majority shade to the Sukkah, and there is not one area of three Tefachim [24 cm.] without Sechach, then the entire Sukkah is valid. The definition of majority shade is that there is more area covered by Sechach than there is empty space.
- <u>Equal amount of empty space and Sechach:</u> If there is an equal amount of empty space and Sechach then the Sukkah is invalid. If, however, one sees an equal amount of sunlight and shade on the ground of the Sukkah then the Sukkah is valid.
- <u>A Sukkah that contains areas with more shade than sunlight and areas with more sunlight than shade:</u> If in total there is more shade than sunlight, then if the area with minority shade is not a size of 7 by 7 Tefachim [56x56 cm], then the entire Sukkah is Kosher, including the area that has minority shade. However, if the majority sunlight area is 7 by 7 Tefachim [56x56 cm], then although the majority shaded area is valid, one may not sit under the area with majority sunlight.
- <u>A Sukkah that contains areas that is not covered [is open to the sky]?</u> If the open area is less than 3x3 Tefach [24x24 cm] it is permitted to eat under the area. If the uncovered area stretches from wall to wall, then if it is three Tefach wide, the Sukkah is considered split in half and is possibly invalid if it will lack three walls due to this. If the uncovered area is adjacent to the walls then if it is three Tefach wide, the adjacent wall is invalidated. This can possibly invalidate the entire Sukkah if the Kosher Sechach will not remain with 3 Kosher walls.
- <u>If the majority sunlight area spreads from wall to wall in a three walled Sukkah is the entire Sukkah invalid due to lacking three walls?</u> Some Poskim leave this matter in question and hence one should not eat in such a Sukkah.
- <u>If the area with majority shade is 20 by 6 Tefachim wide and there is majority shade in total in the Sukkah may one eat under that area?</u> Yes, as only when there is 7 Tefachim in each direction is it not nullified to the majority shade area.

- The Chassidic meaning behind the requirement of majority shade: The Sukkah represents the drawing of an Oar Makif down below, to the Jew dwelling inside. Now an Oar Makif is a very high level of G-dliness [level of Yashis Choshech Sisro] which can only be transmitted in a concealed fashion, hence the requirement for the Sukkah to retain majority shade.

C. Maximum amount of Sechach-Is there a maximum amount of Sechach that may be placed on the Sukkah?

- Allowing the stars to be seen: Initially, the Sechach must be thin and light enough for the large stars to be visible through the Sechach at night. Bedieved, even if the Sechach is as thick as the roof of a house to the point that no rays of sun penetrate the Sechach, the Sukkah is valid so long as rain is able to penetrate through the Sechach, as will be explained next. [The Chabad custom is to make a hole in the Sechach to allow one to see the stars.]
- Allowing rain to penetrate: If the Sechach is thick to the point that even rain is unable to penetrate, it is invalid.
- How much of the Sechach must be able to be penetrated by rain and allow star viewing? Some Poskim rule that so long as the stars are visible from one area within the Sukkah it is initially valid. [Practically, this is the Chabad custom.] However, if rain cannot penetrate in an area of four Tefachim then that area is considered invalid Sechach for all purposes. Others, however, rule that so long as there is a 7x7 area that allows penetration of rain, the entire Sukkah is Kosher.
- Is rain protective Sechach made in a way that it drains the water to outside the Sukkah valid for use? This matter is debated amongst the Poskim.
- The Chassidic meaning behind allowing the stars to be seen: The Sukkah represents the drawing of an Oar Makif down below to the Jew dwelling inside. The purpose of this Oar Makif is to be drawn internally into the Jew. This is represented by the stars which represent a glimmer of the Makif light.

D. Laws relating to Kosher Sechach

- The general ruling: The following criteria is required for a material to be valid Sechach: a) The material grew from the ground. b) The material is currently detached from the ground. c) The material has not been formed into an item which can receive impurity.
- The definition of earth products which are able to contract impurity: Any item that is potentially able to contract impurity is invalid for Sechach. All fruits and vegetables are invalid being that they potentially can contract impurity after having been prepared [by coming in contact with liquids].
- A broken vessel: Any earth produce which was once able to contract impurity due to it being transformed into a vessel, remains Rabbinically invalid even if it has broken and is no longer fit for use as a vessel. If one used this material as Sechach the Sukkah is invalid even Bedieved just like material that is Biblically invalid.
- Earth produce which contain a hole in them: Any produce which had a hole made into them, in a way that they can hold items in that hole, is able to contract impurity and is thus invalid. If the produce grew with this hole, such as a bamboo stick which contains a natural inner hollowness, then it still remains valid.
- Earth produce which lost their original form-Cotton and Cannabis: Any earth produce which changed form, as is the case with cotton and cannabis which have been spun, is Rabbinically invalid. [Regarding using carton boxes and the like-see list]

- Ropes: Based on the above, ropes which are made of materials which were spun in order to firm them, are invalid. However, if they were not spun and the rope is rather made of strings of that material which have retained their original form of growth, then they are valid, as ropes do not have a hole within them to hold items and thus do not contract impurity.

E. List of items and their status:

- May mats be used for Sechach: Mats which are formed from produce that grows from the ground such as bamboo or canes or twigs, may be used for Sechach so long as the following conditions are fulfilled: a) Are not made for any use which would deem it able to contract impurity, such as for sleeping on, spreading fruits on, and the like. b) Not used by majority of the inhabitants of the area as a vessel. c) They are not used in one's area as the roofing for the houses.

- If one does not know the purpose for which a mat was made for then if one bought it from a craftsman for the sake of using as Sechach it is valid [so long as the other conditions are fulfilled] being that the craftsman makes it with the intent of having it used for whatever purpose the consumer chooses to use it for. If, however, one bought it from a private individual then one follows the accustomed use of this item by the majority of the inhabitants of that area. If there is no set custom for this item then one is to follow its size, meaning that if it is small it is assumed to have been made for sleeping on and is thus invalid, while if it is large it is valid unless it has rims around it.

- Practically, must the commonly sold bamboo Sechach mats contain a reliable Rabbinical supervision? Yes. This is due to the fact that in some countries the mats are actually used for roofing or other vessel purpose in which the ruling in Shulchan Aruch dictates that it may then not be used as Sechach. Thus, supervision is required to verify that the mats are not being made for an invalidating purpose. As well, supervision is required to verify that the sticks of the mat are woven using material valid for Sechach, such as the more expensive cotton string, in contrast to the cheaper synthetic strings which are invalid for Sechach.

- A wood ladder: It is questionable whether or not a ladder is deemed to be able to contract impurity, as there is doubt as to whether the side cavities of the ladder in which the steps enter into render it a hole made to hold items or not. Practically one is to be stringent.

- May one use branches that contain fruit as Sechach? If the branches were cut with intent to use as Sechach, they are valid. If, however, they were cut with intent to eat the fruit, then one must have majority of the Sechach be from the part of the branches which is past the area of the stem of the fruit which is able to contract impurity. If the majority is from the area of the stem which can contract impurity, then it is invalid.

- Is plastic a valid material for Sechach? No.

- Is glass a valid material for Sechach? Glass that is produced from sand is Biblically invalid for use as Sechach, being that sand is like earth and does not grow from the ground. However, glass that is made from ash of plants, some Poskim allow using it in a time of need. Others however rule that glass is Rabbinically invalid being it does not provide shade.

- List of items that are invalid to be used as Sechach:
  - Plastic
  - Glass
  - Carton
  - Paper
  - Cotton

- Bamboo mats which did not have a reliable Rabbinical supervision.
- Pieces of wood broken from a chair, bed, bench, dresser, ladder, small container: It is debated in Poskim whether these items are valid or not.
- May one use pieces of Sechach which have been painted over? Yes.
- Does Sechach have Kedushas Shevi'is? No.
- May one cut Sechach during Shemitah to use for his Sukkah? Yes. However, it is best to do so in an irregular method than that used for trimming trees.
- May one's Pergola contain sockets which serve as slots to slide the Sechach into? Yes.

F. If the branch of a tree is resting over one's Sukkah roofing may one simply cut it off and have it used as Sechach?

- No. The Sechach must be originally placed on the roofing at a time that it is currently valid to be used and here since when the branch was placed on the roofing it was still attached to the ground, it is thus invalid. One may however lift the branch after it is cut and then replace it as valid Sechach.

G. Materials which give off bad odors:

- The Sages initially forbade using Sechach which gives off foul odors due to that this may cause one to leave the Sukkah [due to annoyance]. Nevertheless, if one went ahead and used branches which give bad odor as Sechach, the Sukkah is nevertheless valid, and it is even initially permitted to eat in this Sukkah.

H. May branches with leaves be used for Sechach?

- The Sages initially forbade using Sechach which contain leaves that commonly fall off on their own, even without wind, due to suspicion that this may cause one to leave the Sukkah [due to annoyance]. Nevertheless, if one went ahead and used branches which contain leaves as Sechach, the Sukkah is nevertheless valid, and it is even initially permitted to eat in this Sukkah.

I. Bundles of wood and wood boards:

- May bundles of wood be used as Sechach? Bundles of wood which are commonly placed on rooftops for drying purposes [such as those which contain 25 pieces] are Rabbinically invalid for Sechach. However, if the bundle is opened and spread across the Sechach roofing then it is valid.
- May one use wood boards as Sechach? All wooden planks which are slightly wide, similar to a table, and is thus fit to support things, is Rabbinically invalid for Sechach. These planks may not even be used to support the Sechach.
- Boards which are 4 Tefach wide [32 cm.] are Rabbinically invalid to be used as Sechach. Furthermore, today in which even boards of less than 3 Tefach [24 cm] wide are used for roofs of houses, even boards of less than 3 Tefach wide are invalid to be used for Sechach due to the above decree. However, boards which are so narrow that they are not at all used for a roofing are permitted to be used for Sechach, even if they are wide enough to hold fruits and bread. Nevertheless, when such boards are used one must verify that rain is still able to penetrate the Sukkah. For this reason, the custom became to completely avoid using even the valid boards for Sechach due to worry that one may come to set it there in a way that the rain will not be able to penetrate.

- Even if one places a wide board with its width facing upwards, and thus its width <u>over the Sukkah</u> is less than an amount which invalidates, it is nevertheless invalid.
- <u>What is the law if one went ahead and used wood boards as Sechach?</u> If the boards are not wide enough to be used similar to a table [i.e. they are not planks] then even if they are 4 Tefach [32 cm.] wide they are valid, as whenever Sechach is invalidated due to a decree, it is permitted after the fact.

J. If no other Sechach material is available, may one use material which is only Rabbinically invalid?

- Any material which is merely invalidated due to a decree may be used as Sechach if nothing else is available. [However, if it was deemed Rabbinically able to contract impurity, then it is invalid to be used in all cases.]

K. Mamad-Must the items which support the Sechach [The "Mamad"] be themselves kosher for Sechach?

- From the letter of the law, the Sechach may be placed over a wall made of any material, even a material which can contract impurity. However, the Sages decreed that initially the Sechach should only be placed on something which is not able to contract impurity, or on something which one would never come to use as Sechach such as stone wall and the like.
- <u>Must the support of the support [i.e. Maamid Demamid] be of materials valid for Sechach?</u> The Sages never decreed that the support of the supports be made of materials valid for Sechach and thus any material may be used even initially. One may thus make the walls of the Sukkah from materials invalid for Sechach and place over them a material which is valid for Sechach, in order to support the Sechach.
- <u>Nailing the supports of the Sechach:</u> Based on the above that no decree was made against using invalid Sechach to support the support of the Sechach, it is thereby permitted to nail in the supports of the Sechach, or tie them down with material that is invalid for Sechach, as the nail and rope are merely a support of the support.
- <u>If the supports were mistakenly made of material which are invalid for Sechach does the Sukkah remain valid?</u> The Sukkah remains valid, and it is permitted to even initially dwell in such a Sukkah in order to fulfill the Mitzvah.
- <u>May one place items which are invalid for Sechach, over the Sechach to support if from flying away?</u> The decree of the Sages against using for supports items that are invalid for Sechach applies as well to items placed on the Sechach for purpose of weighing it down. [Thus, initially one may not use nails, or rope which is invalid for Sechach, to nail or tie down the Sechach to the Sukkah.]
- <u>Example of items which may not be used to support the Sechach:</u> Metal poles; Plastic rope.
- <u>If there are no valid supports available may an invalid support be used?</u> Yes

L. A Sukkah with areas that do not have Sechach or have invalid Sechach

- <u>May one eat under an area in the Sukkah that is not covered [is open to the sky]?</u> If the area is less than 3x3 Tefach it is permitted to eat under the area. If the uncovered area stretches from wall to wall, then if it is three Tefach wide, the Sukkah is considered split in half and is possibly invalid if it will lack three walls due to this. If the uncovered area is adjacent to the walls, then if it is three Tefach wide, the adjacent wall is invalidated. This can possibly invalidate the entire Sukkah if the Kosher Sechach will not remain with 3 Kosher walls.

- <u>May one eat under an area in the Sukkah that contains invalid Sechach over it?</u> If the invalid Sechach is 4 Tefach [32 cm] wide, and passes **from one end of the Sukkah to another**, it is considered as if the Sukkah is split in half. Thus, if the Sukkah has three walls it is possible for the entire Sukkah to be invalid. If the Sechach is less than 4 Tefach wide, the entire Sukkah is Kosher and one may even eat under the non-Kosher Sechach. However, some rule that if the non-Kosher Sechach is 3 Tefach wide one may not eat under it. Practically one is to initially be stringent and not eat under that area. If the Sechach is less than 3 Tefach wide one may eat under the non-Kosher Sechach according to all opinions.
- If the invalid Sechach is 4 x 4 Tefach [32x32 cm.] wide, then according to all one may not eat under that area. If the area is less than 4x4 it is valid to eat and sleep under it.
- <u>Dofen Akum-If the invalid Sechach is adjacent to the walls of the Sukkah:</u> If the invalid Sechach is adjacent to the walls of the Sukkah then if the invalid Sechach is less than 4 Tefach wide one may even eat under it although practically one is to be stringent if it is 3 Tefach wide. If the invalid Sechach is more than 4 Tefach wide but less than 4 Amos, the Sukkah remains Kosher, as we apply the rule of Dofen Akuma. Nevertheless, one may not eat under the non-Kosher Sechach. If it is more than 4 Amos wide, then the wall that is adjacent to the invalid Sechach is considered non-existent and can possibly invalidate the entire Sukkah if the Kosher Sechach will not remain with 3 Kosher walls. [Some Poskim rule that in order to apply the rule of Dofen Akum the wall must reach the invalid Sechach. If the wall is distanced from the invalid Sechach then it is disputed if we apply the rule of Dofen Akum.]

M. If on Shabbos or Yom Tov the Sechach blew off due to wind may it be replaced?
- No. It is forbidden for a Jew to replace the Sechach. This applies even if only part of the Sechach blew off or folded over one may nevertheless not spread it back onto the Sukkah. If, however, there is no other Sukkah available, one may ask a gentile to replace the Sechach for him.

N. The law if non-Kosher Sechach is mixed together with the Kosher Sechach, or is sitting on top of it:
- We consider the non-Kosher Sechach as nullified when <u>all</u> the following conditions are fulfilled: a) There is enough Kosher Sechach to give majority of shade on its own. b) There is a lot more Kosher Sechach then non-Kosher Sechach. c) The non-Kosher Sechach cannot give majority of shade on its own, or can give majority of shade on its own but there is so much Kosher Sechach that even if one were to remove all the non-Kosher Sechach and an equal amount of Kosher Sechach then the Kosher Sechach would still give majority shade, then it is valid.
- If any of the above conditions are lacking, such as if the Kosher Sechach cannot give majority shade on its own, or can but there is more non-Kosher Sechach than Kosher, or not but there is enough non-Kosher Sechach to give majority of shade on its own, and if one were to remove all the non-Kosher Sechach and an equal amount of Kosher Sechach then the Kosher Sechach would not give majority shade, then it is invalid.

O. The law if Non-Kosher Sechach [Tree or ledge] is hovering over ones Sukkah:

- The shade must come as a result of Kosher Sechach: Just like by the clouds of glory it was the actual clouds which gave us shade from the sun, similarly a Sukkah is only valid when the Kosher Sechach gives the shade. For this reason, one is to verify and remove any interference that rest between the Sechach and the sky, such as a tree which hovers over the Sukkah.

- The law if non-Kosher Sechach hovers over the Sukkah, such as a tree hovering over a Sukkah: The hovered area is considered as if it is not covered by any Sechach, and if due to this the Sukkah would have more sunlight then shade, then the Sukkah is invalid. Although in a case of need, it is better to eat in such a Sukkah than to nullify the Mitzvah.

- Does Non-Kosher Sechach, such as a hovering tree, which is over 20 Amos high, invalidate the Sukkah if the above conditions are not met? Some Poskim rule that it invalidates the Sukkah. Other Poskim rule that when the tree is above 20 Amos, it no longer invalidates the Sechach that is under it.

- If a tree or wall is standing next to ones Sukkah and gives it shade to the point that even if the Sechach were to be gone there would still be shade in the Sukkah, is the Sukkah valid? Yes. So long as the Sechach is directly under the skies, it is valid, irrelevant to whether or not there are other reasons for why there would anyways be shade.

- If a tree near the Sukkah blows with the wind and causes it to hover over the Sukkah, does it invalidate the Sechach under it? No.

- If a hot air balloon or plane, or helicopter hovers over one's Sukkah, does it invalidate the Sechach under it? Yes, it invalidates it according to those Poskim that invalidate the Kosher Sechach even if the hovering is 20 above. However according to those Poskim which are lenient, as explained above, then in this case as well it would be permitted.

- If laundry lines or electric wires hover over ones Sukkah, do they invalidate the Sechach? If the individual lines/wires are not within three Tefachim [24 cm] of each other, then they do not invalidate the Sechach. **If they are within 3 Tefach of each other then:** Some Poskim rule that one is to suspect for the Bach who holds Levud Lehachmir and thus the Sukkah is considered to be under a non-kosher roofing for the entire circumference of the hovering lines. Others however limit this stringency of the Bach to a case where all the hovering items would take up 4 Tefach [32 cm] if they were to be placed adjacent to each other they, which is not the case by lines, and thus in the above scenario it would be permitted according to all.
If there is laundry over the lines: This does not invalidate the Sukkah so long as the laundry is hanging down vertically, as opposed to spread horizontally over the lines. When hanging vertically it is allowed even if the clothing blow with wind and thus at times spread horizontally over the Sukkah. If, however the cloths were spread horizontally, or due to wind got stuck on another line, and are now spread vertically, then that area invalidates the Sechach under it.

- If there is snow on ones Sechach, does it invalidate the Sechach under it? Some Poskim rule that it is a kosher roofing and thus the Sukkah remains valid. Others rule that the Sechach under it is invalidated [and thus if due to this there is not more shade over sunlight within the Sukkah, then the entire Sukkah is invalid]. The Chabad custom follows this stringent opinion even on Shemini Atzeres. One is to thus remove the snow before eating in the Sukkah. On Shabbos one would hint to a gentile to do so for him.

P. Building a Sukkah on/under roof frames and pergolas:

- <u>If the ceiling frame is material Kosher for Sechach</u>: If the ceiling supports are made of material Kosher for Sechach, then one may make the Sukkah under this frame, or place the Sechach over the frame. Furthermore, this frame material itself joins the Kosher Sechach to give majority shade and one may eat directly under it, if one removed the ceiling panels from it in order to replace it with Kosher Sechach.

- <u>When placing Sechach over a pergola, do the boards of the pergola join to become Kosher Sechach</u>? If one did not remove any tiles from the pergola frame for the purpose of building the Sukkah, then the frame remains invalid even if one places Kosher Sechach over the frames. Nevertheless, if the frames are not 3x3 Tefach, then it is permitted to eat under them.

- <u>If the ceiling frame is material not Kosher for Sechach</u>: If the ceiling frame is material not Kosher for Sechach, then the frames invalidate all the Sechach directly under it.

- <u>The law of Lavud by an invalid frame</u>: Even if the roof frames which are invalid for Sechach are within three handbreadths within each other, nevertheless, we do not say the concept of Lavud, and therefore one may eat under the Kosher Sechach. However, with regards to whether one may eat under the actual ceiling supports, this is dependent on whether they are 3x3 Tefach large.

- What is the law if the Sechach is placed on top of an invalid pergola and not in between? If one places Sechach on top of the pergola, it has the same law as Sechach which is placed in between the pergola. Thus, even if the pergola is invalid for Sechach and is within three Tefach of each other, nevertheless the Sukkah is valid, and we do not apply the rule of Lavud.

- If the frames are within three Tefach from each other, is it valid to make the Sukkah <u>under</u> it? It is implied from Admur that if the Sechach is not in between [or in close proximity] to the invalid pergola, then we apply the rule of Lavud.

Q. Building a Sukkah under/over a retractable roof:

- <u>Placing Kosher Sechach under a retractable roof and then removing the roof</u>: If one built a Sukkah inside one's home under a removable roof [prior to opening it], then if one removes the roof from above, then the Sukkah is valid. It does not suffice to simply open the roof and leave it on hinges in a way that it can be opened and closed constantly, but rather the entire roofing must be removed. If, however, the awning was opened at the time that one placed the Sechach on the Sukkah, then even if one later closes the roof, he does not need to completely detach the retractable awning from the Sukkah in order to validate it once again, and rather simply opening the awning validates it. It is thus permitted to close the awning without restriction, and have open it when one desires to be in the Sukkah.

- <u>Retractable Sukkah awnings</u>: It is a Mitzvah to have a retractable Sukkah awning over ones Sukkah in order to prevent the Sechach from getting wet in times of rain, as well as so he be able to stay in the Sukkah even when raining outside. The retractable awning must be opened when one places the Sechach on the Sukkah.

- Some Poskim suggest that it is proper to leave the retractable roof open upon the entrance of Sukkos in order for the Sukkah be valid when the holiness of the holiday penetrates.

- What is one to do if he placed the Sechach under the awning while the awning was closed and it is now Yom Tov? Some Poskim allow one to eat in the Sukkah with a blessing, by simply opening the awning, despite not having removed it or shaken the Sechach [which is not allowed to be done on Yom Tov].

- When one is not eating in the Sukkah should the awning be left opened? Although it is not required from the letter of the law, it is proper to leave the awning opened even at times that one is not found in the Sukkah, with exception to when it rains in which it is proper to close it to prevent wetting ones Sechach.
- If one closed the awning due to rain is there any meaning behind still remaining in the Sukkah? By a wood, plastic, or glass awning within 10 Tefach of the Sechach, which does not have a metal frame: Although there is no requirement to remain in the Sukkah, it is proper to still remain in the Sukkah, as it is presently only Rabbinically invalid due to the awning, however Biblically it remains valid.
- By a metal awning, or an awning above 10 Tefach from the Sechach, or any awning with a metal frame: Then the Sukkah is even Biblically invalid and thus no Mitzvah at all is fulfilled by remaining there. Nevertheless, some have written that it is proper to remain in the Sukkah even then, being that it is a place of holiness.
- On Shabbos or Yom Tov, if rainwater has gathered over one's awning or Sechach covering, may it be removed if it will subsequently cause the water to fall onto earth or grass and the like? If the ground is already anyways very wet due to the rain, then one may be lenient to remove the covering, having the water fall on the ground. If, however, it is not very wet then it is forbidden to be done due to a possible planting prohibition.
- If it is raining on Yom Tov may one place a sheet or the like over or under the Sechach? Yes, as long as the sheet is not distanced more than a Tefach from the Sechach, in order so one not transgress the prohibition of making an Ohel on Yom Tov.
- On Shabbos and Yom Tov, may one open or close the retractable awning of a Sukkah? If the retractable awning of the Sukkah has hinges with which it is opened and closed, then it is like a door and is permitted to be opened and closed on Shabbos and Yom Tov and doing so does not contain the Building or destroying prohibition. However, this only applies if the awning rests within a Tefach of the Sechach when it is closed. However, if there is a Tefach between the roofing and the Sechach then it is forbidden to be opened or closed due to the Ohel prohibition.
- Placing Kosher Sechach over non-Kosher Sechach and then removing the non-Kosher Sechach: If one placed Kosher Sechach over non-Kosher Sechach and then removed the non-Kosher Sechach from under the Kosher Sechach, the Sukkah is invalid due to the rule of Taaseh Velo Min Hasuiy. Therefore, when placing the Sechach one is required to have nothing intervening between it and the Sukkah. If one did not do so, then after the non-Kosher Sechach is removed, the Kosher Sechach must also be removed and then replaced.

R. A two story Sukkah:
- If one built a Sukkah on top of another Sukkah then if the floor of the top Sukkah, which serves also as the Sechach for the top Sukkah, is able to support pillows and blankets [and a person eating and sleeping], then although the top Sukkah is valid, the bottom Sukkah is invalid.
- May one have a Sukkah made with two layers of Sechach one over the other? If the two layers of Sechach are ten or more Tefach [80cm.] apart, and the lower Sechach is sturdy enough to support pillows and blankets, then it is viewed as a two-story Sukkah and the Sukkah is thus invalid.
- May one eat in a Sukkah which has the Sechach of an upper Sukkah protruding over it? If the bottom Sechach is firm enough to hold a person lying on pillows and blankets: This matter is

disputed by Poskim. Some Poskim hold that it does not invalidate the Sechach directly under it being that this protruding Sechach has no walls. Others, however, rule that despite the above it does invalidate the Sechach under it. Practically, one is to be stringent and avoid this situation. If the bottom Sechach cannot hold a person lying on a pillow: The lower Sukkah is completely valid.

S. Items hovering between one's head and the Sechach

*   A flat hovering which is a handbreadth wide [8 cm.], or contains one Tefach of width within three Tefach of height, and has a height of 10 handbreadths [80 cm.] from the ground, has the legal status of a tent and it is thus forbidden for one to eat or sleep under it.
*   May one eat or sleep under the table or chair in the Sukkah? So long as the table or chair does not reach a height of ten Tefach [80 cm.] then it is permitted to even initially sleep or eat under it. [Nevertheless, it is best to sleep and eat directly under the Sechach then under a hovering, even if less than 10 Tefach high.]
*   May one sleep on a bunk bed? The top bed is within 10 Tefach [80 cm.] from the ground: Then it is disputed amongst Poskim whether one may sleep on the lower bed which is hovered over by the upper bed. Some Poskim rule that it is forbidden, similar to the ruling regarding a bed canopy in which it was ruled that it is forbidden to sleep on such a bed even if the canopy does not reach 10 Tefach from above the ground. Other Poskim however permit sleeping on the lower bed based on a differentiation between this case, in which the upper bed is only placed there due to lack of space, and the case of the canopy, in which the canopy is purposely placed to hover the bed as part of the beds furniture, and thus in the former case no decree of the Sages was made.
*   The bed is higher than 10 Tefach from the ground: It is forbidden to sleep on the lower bed.
*   Having a decorations and decorative sheet under one's Sechach: If a decorative sheet is spread under one's Sechach for purposes of beautification of the Sukkah, then if it is within 4 Tefach [32 cm.] from the Sechach, it is nullified to the Sukkah and one may eat under it. This applies even if the sheet is 4 Tefach wide [32 cm.] and is a height of 10 Tefach from above ground. However, if the sheet reaches below 4 Tefach [32 cm.] from the Sechach then it is defined as invalid Sechach. Even if the sheet is less than 4 Tefach wide, it may not be placed below 4 Tefach from the Sechach due to a decree that one may come to do so with a sheet that is 4 Tefach wide.
*   May one eat under a protruding decoration which was placed on one's wall? If the decoration is within 4 Tefach from the Sechach then it is nullified to the Sechach and one may thus eat under it. If, however, it is below 4 Tefach from the Sechach then it is forbidden to eat under it.
*   May one place decorations within four Tefach from the Sechach if they reach below 4 Tefach from ones Sechach? This is to be avoided due to it being questionable whether or not this decoration is nullified to the Sechach and hence perhaps it is an interval between the person and the Sechach. However, there are Poskim which are lenient in this matter so long as the top of the decoration is within four Tefach from the Sechach. Practically, it should be avoided.
*   Having a sheet placed in order to catch leaves, bugs or rain: If a sheet was placed under the Sechach to catch leaves or rain and the like it is disputed whether or not the sheet is nullified to the Sechach. Practically, at times of rain it is better to place a sheet over or under the Sechach, and prevent rain from entering, then to go inside the house.

3. The Mitzvah of dwelling in a Sukkah

A. The Mitzvah:

- The Torah commands us to dwell in a Sukkah for seven days from the 15th of Tishrei through the 21st of Tishrei. This Mitzvah is a positive Biblical command and is fulfilled every moment that one dwells in the Sukkah.
- The reason behind the Mitzvah: The verse states that the reason Hashem commanded us to dwell in a Sukkah is in order "Lemaan Yeidu Doroseichem Ki Besukkos Hoshavti Es Bnei Yisrael Behotzi Osam Me'eretz Mitzrayim." This refers to the clouds of glory [Ananei Hakavod] which Hashem surrounded us with for the sake of shade, so we are not exposed to heat waves and the sun. In replica of this, Hashem commanded us to make Sukkos for the sake of shade, in order so we recall the miracles and wonders [he performed for us in the desert].
- No quarrels in home: One who is careful in the Mitzvah of Sukkah, and makes it properly, is guaranteed to not suffer from quarrels and fights amongst his household for the entire year.
- May one eat and drink in the Sukkah on Erev Sukkos? Yes.
- Kissing the Sukkah: Some are accustomed to also kiss the Sukkah upon entering and exiting to show their belovedness of the Mitzvah.

B. The Kavana when dwelling in the Sukkah:

- The reason G-d commanded us to dwell in a Sukkah is so we recall the miracles and wonders done for us in the desert, in which the clouds of glory surrounded us for shade, as protection from the sun. Thus, every person must have in mind when dwelling in a Sukkah, that he is dwelling in it in order to fulfill G-d's command to sit in a Sukkah in commemoration of the Exodus. [One is to think of the exodus, the clouds of glory, and the general miracles and wonders that Hashem performed for us. It does not suffice to merely think about the exodus in passing thought, but rather the main point is for one to contemplate it.]
- If one did not have the above Kavana upon dwelling in the Sukkah, does he fulfill his obligation? Some Poskim rule that one who does not have the above-mentioned intent upon dwelling in the Sukkah, does not fulfill the Mitzvah. Other Poskim rule that although one has certainly not fulfilled the command properly, nonetheless, he does fulfill his obligation.
- Prior to fulfilling any Mitzvah, one must intend to perform it in order to fulfill the command of Hashem. One who dwells in a Sukkah without even this intent, does not fulfill the Mitzvah at all.
- Must one have this intent every time he dwells in the Sukkah? Yes. Each time one eats in the Sukkah, and fulfills the Mitzvah of dwelling in the Sukkah, he is to intend to fulfill the Mitzvah for the above-mentioned reason of commemorating the exodus.

C. Who is obligated:

- Women: Women are exempt from dwelling in the Sukkah. However, if a woman desires to dwell in the Sukkah, she may do so. [Unlike the Mitzvah of Lulav and Shofar, women did not accept upon themselves the Mitzvah of Sukkah, and it hence remains completely optional. Nonetheless, it is a Mitzvah on the husband to have his family, wife and daughters join him in the Sukkah so he fulfills the Mitzvah of dwelling just like in his home, and have them merit the holiness of the Sukkah.]
- The blessing: A woman [of Ashkenazi origin] who dwells in a Sukkah may choose to recite a blessing prior to doing so, just as a man recites prior to performing the Mitzvah. If,

however, a woman does not know how to say the blessing, then a man who already said the blessing of Leisheiv Basukkah on his own behalf, may not repeat the blessing of Leisheiv Basukkah on behalf of the woman. [A blessing may only be recited at certain times, and therefore, it is imperative for women who desire to say a blessing to be aware of the laws involved of when a blessing may and may not be said.]

- Children: [Male] Children which have reached the age of Chinuch are Rabbinically obligated to be educated to eat in the Sukkah. This is defined as when the [male] child no longer needs his mother which is generally from six years old. If the child is sharp and advanced to the point that he does not need his mother even before six years old, then he is obligated to be educated in the Mitzvah of Sukkah. It is the father's obligation to educate this child to dwell in the Sukkah and if he sees him not doing so he must protest his actions and enter him into the Sukkah. However, the mother, and others, are not obligated to educate the child to dwell in the Sukkah and she may even present him a meal outside of the Sukkah so long as she does not tell him to eat outside the Sukkah.
- Must a child be educated to sleep in the Sukkah? A child is to be educated to sleep in the Sukkah. If, however, it is cold outside, then there is no need to do so.
- Should one educate a child to eat all foods in the Sukkah? There is no obligation to do so.
- If a child turns Bar Mitzvah during Sukkos should he say Shehechiyanu? It is proper for the child to say Shehechiyanu on a new fruit while in the Sukkah.
- Chasan: In today's times, a Chasan, and his entourage, are obligated in the Mitzvah of Sukkah throughout the Sheva Brachos just like anyone else. [He is to say a blessing upon eating a meal in the Sukkah, just like any other person.]
- Avel: A mourner is obligated to remove his sadness and dwell in the Sukkah during Sukkos. However, if he is unable to remove the sadness and he needs privacy and seclusion at home in order to handle the mourning, then he is exempt from the Mitzvah.
- Onen: An Onen on Erev Sukkos may build the Sukkah if there is no one else available to do so for him. An Onen is obligated to dwell in the Sukkah during Yom Tov and is to recite a blessing. However, on Chol Hamoed, some Poskim rule the Onen is not obligated to dwell in the Sukkah. Other Poskim, however, rule he is obligated to dwell in the Sukkah. Practically, he is to eat in the Sukkah without a blessing.

D. The Mitzvah of dwelling:

- The definition of dwelling: The verse states "Besukkos Teishvu Shivas Yamim." The Sages received in an oral tradition that this means "Teishvu Keiyn Taduru", that one is to make one's Sukkah his permanent residence and his house temporary for the duration of the festival. This means one must eat, drink, read, learn, socialize, and simply spend time of relaxation [i.e. "Yitayel"] within the Sukkah throughout all seven days both by night and day. If one needs to have a conversation with a friend, he is to do so in the Sukkah. The general rule is a person should act as if his Sukkah is his house, and anything that one would not do outside his house he should not do outside the Sukkah.

E. Eating and drinking in the Sukkah:

- Eating in the Sukkah: One is only required to eat a set meal inside a Sukkah. However, it is permitted to eat a snack outside the Sukkah. The definition of a snack is a Kibeitza or less of bread or Mezonos, and any amount of any other food. This applies even if one makes a set meal on other foods, nevertheless he is not required to eat them in a Sukkah. Thus, one is only required to eat in the Sukkah if he is eating more than a Kibeitza of bread [without the shell, which is more than 53.8 grams] or Mezonos [within Kdei Achilas Pras, which is within 4 minutes].

- Must one eat a meal of Hamotzi or Mezonos in the Sukkah every day? There is no maximum or minimum amount of meals that one must eat in the Sukkah. Thus, if one desires to eat only foods that are not obligated to be eaten in a Sukkah throughout Sukkahs, he may do so. However, this only applies on Chol Hamoed, however on Shabbos and Yom Tov, since according to some opinions one is obligated to eat a Kibeitza of bread for the Shabbos and Yom Tov meal, therefore he must eat these meals in the Sukkah. Furthermore, on the first night of Sukkos, according to all opinions, one must eat at least a Kezayis of bread in the Sukkah. This applies even if it is raining on the first night, although in such a case he is not to say a blessing of Leisheiv Basukkah. [However, the custom of Chassidim is to always recite the blessing.] On the second night of Sukkos in the Diaspora one is not required to eat a Kezayis in the Sukkah if it is raining, although one who desires to be stringent, may do so.
- Drinking in the Sukkah: [From the letter of the law] it is permitted to drink all beverages outside the Sukkah, including wine. One may drink even more than a Revius. This allowance however only applies by a regular drink, however, to settle oneself down on a beverage such as wine or beer or mead, this must be done in the Sukkah as will be explained!
- [The above is only from the letter of the law, however] one who is stringent upon himself to not drink even water outside the Sukkah is praised. [Practically, the Chabad custom is that those who are meticulous do not drink even water outside the Sukkah, even on Shemini Atzeres.]
- Settling oneself over the beverage: One who settles himself down to drink wine, or other beverage of significance of which is it is common to settle oneself upon, is obligated to drink it in the Sukkah. However, the blessing of Leisheiv Basukkah is not said upon drinking it, [with exception to Kiddush and Havdalah in which it is said]. Due to this, that no blessing is said, it is proper not to drink wine, or other significant beverages, in a settling manner in a Sukkah which one has not, and does not plan to, say in it Leisheiv Basukkah that day. [Hence when invited to someone else's Sukkah to settle with him and drink wine, one is to eat a Kibeitza of Mezonos in order so the blessing of Leisheiv Basukkah covers the wine.] However, when eating in a Sukkah that one has said Leisheiv that day, or plans on doing so, then there is no need to refrain from drinking the wine, as it is already included in the blessing of Leisheiv which was, or will, be said that day.
- Drinking the beverage casually: It is permitted from the letter of the law to drink wine or other significant beverages in an unsettling manner outside of the Sukkah. This applies even if one drinks a lot more than a Revius of the beverage. However, one who is stringent to not even drink water outside the Sukkah, is blessed.
- Kiddush: Kiddush is to be made inside the Sukkah. The blessing of Leisheiv Basukkah is said prior to drinking the wine. However, on the 1st night of Sukkos it is said before the blessing of Shehechiyanu, while on the 2nd night it is said after the blessing of Shehechiyanu. [During the day Kiddush, the blessing of Leisheiv is said after the blessing of Hagafen, prior to drinking from the wine.]
- Havdalah: One is obligated to say Havdalah inside the Sukkah. One says the blessing of Leisheiv Basukkah after Havdalah prior to drinking from the wine.

- Must one who is stringent not to even drink water outside a Sukkah, swallow medicine inside a Sukkah? The custom of the Rebbe Rashab was to be stringent to even swallow medicine within the Sukkah.

- Must one who is stringent not to even drink water outside a Sukkah, drink water while traveling if he is very thirsty? It is praiseworthy and an act of piety to be meticulous even in such a case and avoid drinking until one enters a Sukkah. Nevertheless, if this will cause one to fast past midday then he is to drink or eat something.

- May one make Havdalah outside a Sukkah for an ill patient which cannot come into the Sukkah? If the patient is unable to make Havdalah himself then one may do so for him, although he should try to drink only the majority of a Revius, as opposed to a full Revius.

F. Learning and Davening in a Sukkah:

- One must learn Torah inside the Sukkah. (However, if he is learning inside the Beis Midrash he is not required to enter the Sukkah). Likewise, if by learning outside one is able to delve into the subject and understand it in greater depth then he may learn outside the Sukkah in order so he have a more serene mind, as the air of the outside is good for a person to refresh his mind. Nevertheless, it all depends on the situation, as if he is able to learn comfortably in his Sukkah then he must do so.

- If he requires many Sefarim for his learning, then if he is able to make space in his Sukkah in a way that he is not required to remove the Sefarim from the Sukkah during the meals and upon sleeping, then he must set up the Sefarim in his Sukkah and learn in the Sukkah. However, if he is unable to easily prepare an area for the Sefarim and it takes a lot of trouble to remove the Sefarim during the mealtimes and then return them afterwards then he may learn outside the Sukkah.

- Davening in a Sukkah: If one is unable to Daven in Shul, then if he is able to Daven in his Sukkah without disturbances and with a clear mind and proper concentration, he must do so. This however only applies if he is unable to go to Shul, however if he is able to go to Shul then he must do so and is not required to Daven in his Sukkah. If he is unable to Daven with concentration in his Sukkah then he may Daven inside his house.

- Shaking Lulav in the Sukkah: From the letter of the law, one is to fulfill the Mitzvah of shaking Lulav before Hallel. However, since it is a Mitzvah Min Hamuvchar to shake the Lulav in the Sukkah, and one cannot leave the Shul in the interim due to the onlookers, therefore in the morning, prior to prayer, one is to say the blessing over the Lulav while still in the Sukkah.

- Must a Bris Mila take place in a Sukkah? Yes.

G. Sleeping in Sukkah:

- The obligation-Letter of the law: Part of the Mitzvah and [Biblical] obligation of dwelling in a Sukkah, is to sleep in the Sukkah throughout all seven days of Sukkos, both by day and night, just as one does in his home throughout the year. It is forbidden to sleep outside of a Sukkah, even for a mere nap. Despite this obligation and prohibition, today the custom of the world is to be lenient and not to sleep in the Sukkah, with exception to those who are meticulous in Mitzvos. [Likewise, the Chabad practice is not to sleep in the Sukkah, due to reasons to be explained.] The following are the cases of exceptions and reasons of leniency for why many no longer sleep in the Sukkah:

- Rain: During times of rain, even if it is only a mere drizzle, one is not obligated to sleep in the Sukkah, being that it is uncomfortable to sleep there. If the rain stopped, then if he did not yet lie down to go to sleep in his home, he is obligated to return to sleep in the Sukkah. If, however, he already laid down in his house to go to sleep, then he is not required to return to the Sukkah. However, once it is past Alos then if one wakes up and notices the rain has ended, he must return to the Sukkah if he desires to continue sleeping.
- Insects-Mosquitos: If one is disturbed by mosquitos in the Sukkah, he is exempt from sleeping in the Sukkah.
- Hot weather: During times of heat, one is not obligated to sleep in the Sukkah, if it is uncomfortable to sleep there.
- Cold weather: In cold climate areas, in which it is painful [i.e. uncomfortable] to sleep inside the Sukkah, and one does not own enough blankets and sheets to properly warm himself up, then he is not obligated to sleep inside the Sukkah. [If he does own warm enough blankets to protect him from the cold inside the Sukkah, then he must enter them into the Sukkah and sleep there, unless one of the following other exceptions apply.]
- Not enough room in the Sukkah for a bed: Even if one owns enough blankets to keep him warm in the Sukkah, if [the Sukkah is small and] one is unable to set up his sleeping quarters in the Sukkah for all seven days of the festival, in a way that he will not need to remove the [bed and] sleeping accessories from the Sukkah during meal times [in order to make space], then he is exempt from sleeping in his Sukkah. This however only applies if removing and setting up the sleeping quarters [daily] is considered an extra burden, and one is distressed by this burden to the point that if he had such a burden in his home he would not [enter the bed and accessories into the bedroom and] sleep there [but would rather sleep in the room that the bed and accessories are currently located in].
- One who is married: Some Poskim suggest, in defense of those who do not sleep in the Sukkah, that a married man is exempt from sleeping in the Sukkah [at night] if he desires to sleep with his wife in the same room [and his wife does not want to sleep in the Sukkah, or the Sukkah does not provide enough privacy]. This applies even if his wife is a Nida. This exemption applies during the nighttime [however not during the day]. Nevertheless, [despite the above suggestive justification] it is proper to be stringent to build a private Sukkah in which one is able to sleep there [even at night] together with his wife.
- Noise: One who is unable to sleep in his Sukkah due to noise, is exempt from doing so and may sleep in his home.
- The custom today: Today, the custom of the world is to be lenient and not sleep in the Sukkah [and so is the Chabad custom], with exception to those who are meticulous in Mitzvos. Some have learned merit for their practice based on the fact that [it is too cold to sleep in the Sukkah, or alternatively] regarding married men, due to the fact a married person may sleep at home with his wife [as explained above].
- The Chabad custom: The custom of many Chabad Chassidim is not to sleep in the Sukkah even if one of the above listed exceptions do not apply, due to the reason to be explained below. This custom dates back to the Alter Rebbe, and was instructed by the Mittler Rebbe to the Chassidim. The Rebbe, Rebbe Rayatz and Rebbe Rashab did not sleep in the Sukkah, but rather at home. This custom was also practiced by other Chassidic groups and Chassidic masters, who followed the ways of the Baal Shem Tov. This was the widespread custom of the world in the times of the Rama, as quoted above. Nonetheless, despite this custom and its justification, there are Chabad Chassidim who sleep in the Sukkah, and the Rebbe instructed

that those who did so until this point are to continue to do so despite the custom and its justification. Furthermore, the Rebbe instructed that one may only follow the custom to not sleep in the Sukkah if the reason to be explained is applicable to him, or if one of the other previous mentioned exceptions apply to him. However, one who feels that the reason to be explained is not applicable to him, and also does not have any of the other exceptions apply to him, is obligated to sleep in the Sukkah as is required from the letter of the law, even if he is a Chabad Chassid. [Unfortunately, some have understood the Chabad custom to dismiss the obligation of sleeping in a Sukkah, or even prohibit it, altogether. This is clearly a distortion of the custom, and the intents of those who justified it. In addition, some troubled individuals have unfortunately used this custom as a platform to attack the legitimacy of Chabad Chassidim, and spread slander, baseless hatred and transgress various prohibitions of the Torah, which are too many to enumerate. The custom has clear Halachic basis, was defended and instructed by the greatest of Poskim, and was practiced by all Jewry for one reason or another. Those who attack the custom are in truth attacking all those Poskim and the longstanding tradition of Jewry.]

- The reason and application: The reason behind the custom is due to another aspect of the exception of Mitztaer/distress, which exempts one from sleeping in the Sukkah, and was not listed above. This aspect of Mitztaer is explained as follows: The Sukkah contains a sublime level of holiness, or G-dly revelation, called Makifim Debina. Chabad Chassidus emphasizes the study of Chassidus which internalizes the knowledge of the above level of Divinity. One who has knowledge of this holiness contained in a Sukkah, will naturally be disturbed to perform any action that is unbefitting of the holiness it contains. Now, since during sleep one is unable to be conscious of the holiness of the Sukkah, as well as the act of sleep in it of itself can be viewed as a disrespect to the holiness of the Sukkah, therefore there is distress involved in sleeping in the Sukkah. Accordingly, since sleeping in the Sukkah causes one spiritual pain, he is exempt from doing so, as anyone who is in pain upon dwelling in the Sukkah is exempt from the Mitzvah. This reason especially applies to those Tzaddikim and Chassidim who are on a level that they could feel the holiness of the Sukkah, and therefore simply cannot fall asleep. Furthermore, it even applies to those who do not feel this level of holiness, if they are nevertheless distressed over the fact that they know it contains this holiness, and are disturbed to act in a disrespectful way towards it, such as to sleep in it. Furthermore, it even applies to those who are not disturbed to sleep in the Sukkah due the holiness of the Sukkah, but simply due to the fact that this is the custom of their Rebbe, and they are distressed to not follow in their Rebbe's custom. As stated above, if none of these reasons, or other exceptions, are applicable, and one hence finds no disturbance at all in his sleeping in the Sukkah, then he is obligated to do so.
- If one fears sleeping in the Sukkah due to getting his house robbed, may he sleep at home? Yes.
- Must one sleep in the Sukkah if he needs to care for children at home, such as a single father, or if his wife is away? He is exempt from sleeping in the Sukkah.
- May one who is traveling on a plane or bus fall asleep there? Yes.
- May one learning in the Beis Midrash put his head down for a short nap? Yes.
- May one sleep alone in a Sukkah? Yes.
- May one wash Neigal Vassar in the morning inside the Sukkah? Yes.

H. Items to enter into the Sukkah:

- The table: One must enter a table into his eating Sukkah. One who does so does not fulfill his obligation as we suspect one may come after his food.
- May part of the table be inside the house? Some Poskim require at least a Tefach of the table to be inside the Sukkah in which case it is valid. Others require that majority of the table be inside the Sukkah.
- Vessels: One should enter his most beautiful vessels, tapestries, and drinking utensils into the Sukkah. However, one is not to enter flour vessels and other vessels that are normally not left out within the house. Pots, pans and plates are to be removed from the Sukkah after they are used being that they are repulsive, and it is belittling to the Sukkah. [The custom is not to enter pots into the Sukkah at all and rather the food is to be placed in a serving tray.]
- Entering pots into a Sukkah: [It is permitted to enter pots and pans of food into a Sukkah.] Nonetheless, once the meal has been completed, one is to remove the pots, pans, and plates from the Sukkah, being that after their use they are considered repulsive [and it is belittling to the Sukkah to have them remain]. [According to some opinions, leaving dirty pots and plates in a Sukkah can invalidate the Sukkah, and it is hence to be removed immediately after the meal is completed. The above allowance to initially bring pots of food into a Sukkah is from the letter of the law, however, many Poskim record that the custom is not to enter pots and pans of food into a Sukkah at all even for the purpose of serving the food, and rather the food is served in a dish a tray. However, if there are no plates available, and one needs to eat directly from the pot, then one may enter it into the Sukkah.]
- Candles: One must have light in his Sukkah and thus he is to enter candles in the Sukkah. If they are a fire hazard one may not bring it into the Sukkah even if it is made of gold. One may not enter earthenware candles into his Sukkah [due to it being repulsive].

I. Belittling acts in the Sukkah:

- One may not do any belittling acts inside the Sukkah. Thus, one may not clean the dishes inside the Sukkah, although drinking cups may be washed down.
- May one use a Sukkah as a short cut? No. One is not to make his Sukkah into a shortcut to reach another area.
- May one hang laundry in the Sukkah? No.
- May one allow a gentile to enter one's Sukkah? One should not invite a gentile into the Sukkah as this causes the holiness to leave. Therefore, one should not have a gentile maid clean the Sukkah inside.
- May one have marital relations in a Sukkah? Some Poskim rule it is permitted. Other Poskim however rule it is forbidden have marital relations in the Sukkah.
- May one wash Neigal Vassar inside the Sukkah? Yes.

J. The blessing of Leisheiv Basukkah

- When is the blessing of Leisheiv said? The blessing of 'Leisheiv Basukkah' is only said when eating a Kibeitza [53.8 grams] of Mezonos or Hamotzi [within Kdei Achilas Pras, which is within 4 minutes]. It is not said prior to other actions of dwelling such as a set drinking session, or spending time of leisure or sleeping in the Sukkah [with exception to a Sukkah in which one will not be eating, as explained below].
- Is the blessing of Leisheiv Basukkah said before or after the blessing over food? The blessing of Leisheiv is recited after saying the blessing of the food, but prior to eating it. Thus, if one

eats bread, he first says Hamotzi and then say Leisheiv and then eat. If he is eating a Kibeitza of Mezonos he first says Mezonos, then Leisheiv and then eats the Mezonos. [The Rebbe's custom is to look at Sechach upon saying Leisheiv.]

- How often does one say the blessing of Leisheiv over eating in a Sukkah: Every time one eats a Kibeitza of Mezonos or Hamotzi in the Sukkah he is to say a blessing of Leisheiv Basukkah, if there was an interval between the previous time he ate and the current eating. If, however, no interval was made then he does not repeat the blessing, as the previous blessing still covers his current eating. This applies even if one remained in the Sukkah throughout all seven days of Sukkos without an interval, in which case he would only say the blessing on the first meal he eats in the Sukkah. The definition of an interval is either intent or time. This means as follows: If one left the Sukkah after eating and had intent to not return within one to two hours then even if he returns immediately, he must repeat the blessing prior to eating a Kibeitza of Mezonos. Likewise, even if one intended to return within one to two hours, but in actuality returned after one to two hours, then it is considered an interval and he must repeat the blessing prior to eating a Kibeitza of Mezonos.

- Must one repeat the blessing of Leisheiv Basukkah when eating in a second Sukkah? One must say the blessing of Leisheiv in every Sukkah that he eats a Kibeitza of Mezonos. This applies even if he had in mind to eat in the second Sukkah at the time he began eating in the first Sukkah, and applies even if both Sukkahs are next to each other and a new first blessing is not required to be repeated, nevertheless a new blessing must be said.

- Saying the blessing of Leisheiv on simply relaxing or sleeping in someone else's Sukkah: If one enters into someone else's Sukkah in order to spend time of leisure, or in order to sleep in it, and he does not plan to eat a Kibeitza worth of Mezonos in that Sukkah then he must say the blessing of Leisheiv Basukkah prior to relaxing or sleeping in it. However, if one plans on eating a Kibeitza of Mezonos in that Sukkah, or if he already ate a Kibeitza there, then these acts are exempt with the blessing made on the food.

- If one forgot to say Leisheiv before eating: If one forgot to recite Leisheiv Basukkah prior to eating he is to say it upon remembering. If he has already finished eating and then remembered to say the blessing, then if he is still in the Sukkah, he is to say the blessing upon remembering [even if he has already Bentched].

1. The laws of Mitztaer:

- General Rule: One is only obligated to dwell in his Sukkah in the same matter that he would dwell in his home. Thus, one who is pained to dwell in his Sukkah and through leaving the Sukkah he will be saved from this pain, then he is exempt from dwelling. This however is with exception to the first night of Sukkos in which case one is obligated to eat at least a Kezayis in the Sukkah.

- Dwelling in the Sukkah when one is exempt due to the law of Mitztaer? Anyone who is exempt from dwelling in a Sukkah [due to experiencing pain or distress due to the dwelling] and does not leave the Sukkah, does not receive any reward for that dwelling and is considered a Hedyot [i.e. a fool or ignoramus, or simpleton]. [It is thus certainly forbidden to be stringent and say a blessing upon dwelling in a Sukkah at a time that one is exempt. The above is the letter of the law. However, the custom Chassidim, based on the Baal Shem Tov, is to always eat in the Sukkah even during rain. It is disputed whether one is to say the blessing of Leisheiv Basukkah when eating there during rain. Practically, the Chabad custom is to say a blessing even in the rain.]

- How to leave the Sukkah when Mitztaer: One who leaves his Sukkah due to rain [or other case of distress] is not to [leave angrily and] kick [the Sukkah] but is rather to leave with humility, viewing himself like a slave who served a cup of wine to his master and the master pours it on his face, meaning to say "I am not interested in your service."
- Matters which cause pain and discomfort: Wind; Flies; Gnats; Foul odor.
- Initially building a Sukkah in an area with discomfort: It is forbidden to initially build a Sukkah in an area that one knows contains discomfort that will exempt him from dwelling there. This applies whether the discomfort exempts him from eating there, or sleeping there, or spending time there. If one built a Sukkah in such an area it is invalid. For example, if one built a Sukkah in an area that wind blows in a way that causes one discomfort to eat there, the Sukkah is invalid. Similarly, if one built a Sukkah in the middle of the street and he fears sleeping there due to robbers, the Sukkah is invalid. If, however he does not fear from robbers even though he fears his items will be stolen, the Sukkah remains valid, as he is able to enter these items into his house and then sleep in the Sukkah.
- Matters which only cause discomfort to a minority of individuals: A person that receives discomfort from a matter that most people are not commonly discomforted from, then he must dwell in the Sukkah despite the discomfort, as we follow the common way of living. However, if one knows himself to be a very sensitive and pampered individual in a way that all sensitive and pampered individuals are likewise discomforted by it, then he is exempt from dwelling in the Sukkah.
- Dwelling in a Sukkah during rain: If it rains in one's Sukkah to the point that one's food would become ruined; he is exempt from eating in the Sukkah. This applies even if he currently does not have any food in the Sukkah. This applies even if only a very delicate food [such as Pol-fava bean] would be ruined by the rain. If one is unsure of whether the rain would ruin this food then if it is raining to the point that one would leave his house if this occurred in his house, then he is exempt from Sukkah. On the first night one is to eat a Kezayis of bread in the Sukkah even if it is raining although he is not to say a blessing of Leisheiv Basukkah. On the second night of Sukkos in the Diaspora one is not required to eat a Kezayis in the Sukkah if it is raining although one who desires to be stringent may do so. [The above is the letter of the law however it is the custom Chassidim, based on the Baal Shem Tov, is to always eat in the Sukkah even during rain. It is disputed whether one is to say the blessing of Leisheiv Basukkah when eating there during rain. Practically the Chabad custom is to say a blessing even in the rain.]
- Sleeping: If it is raining in the Sukkah even slightly one is exempt from sleeping there and may sleep outside the Sukkah.
- If one left the Sukkah due to rain and it then stopped raining: If one left the Sukkah in midst of a meal due to the rain and it then stopped raining, he is not required to return to the Sukkah and may rather finish the meal in his house. If one was sleeping in the Sukkah and he left due to rain and it stopped raining before he had a chance to lie down in his bed in his house, then he must return to his Sukkah. If, however one already lied down to go to sleep then he is not required to return to the Sukkah. This applies even if one woke up in middle of the night and realized the rain stopped, nevertheless one is not required to return to the Sukkah to sleep. However, once it is past Alos then if one wakes up and notices the rain has ended, he must return to the Sukkah if he desires to continue sleeping. However, others are not obligated to wake him up past Alos.
- Dwelling in a Sukkah heat wave: If one is experiencing very hot weather in the Sukkah and

one is in pain, he is exempt from dwelling in the Sukkah. This applies even if one's food would not become spoiled due to the heat.

- <u>Dwelling in a Sukkah that contains many insects</u>: If one is experiencing an insect infestation in the Sukkah and one is in pain, he is exempt from dwelling in the Sukkah. This applies even if one's food would not become spoiled due to the insects.
- <u>Dwelling in a Sukkah during very cold weather</u>: If one is experiencing very cold weather in the Sukkah to the point that his fatty foods congeal, he is exempt from dwelling in the Sukkah.
- <u>Eating in a Sukkah that does not have light</u>: If the lights extinguished within the Sukkah during Shabbos of the festival, and he contains light within his house, then he is permitted to leave his Sukkah and eat in his house near the light. One is not obligated to enter into another person's Sukkah which contains light in order to eat there, as this is also painful for a person to require him to eat his meal in another person's home. Nevertheless, if one is able to enter another person's Sukkah without great difficulty, then he is to do so and is not to be lenient in this matter.

K. One who is traveling:

- One who is traveling during the holiday of Sukkos through in an uninhabited area and is sleeping and eating in the fields, is exempt from building a Sukkah. However, when he arrives to a town, even a town of gentiles, and he desires to eat or sleep there, he must build a Sukkah if he has time to build it prior to the normal time one eats and sleeps.
- <u>One who is traveling for a Mitzvah</u>: If one is traveling for a Mitzvah purpose, such as to redeem a captive or to greet his Rebbe, then he is not required to dwell in the Sukkah during his travels even if he is in an inhabited area that contains a Sukkah. However, if the Sukkah is near him, and he is able to dwell in the Sukkah without any impediments being caused to the fulfillment of the Mitzvah, then he is to dwell in the Sukkah.
- <u>May one travel for leisure purposes, like going on an overnight hike, if there will not be a Sukkah available during their stay?</u> One may not do so. One may only travel through areas without a Sukkah for business purposes or other necessary purposes.

L. City guards:

- Guards of a city, which surveillance the city for enemy attacks, are exempt from dwelling or eating in a Sukkah during their time of surveillance. However, after their duty is over, they are obligated to eat in a Sukkah.
- <u>Does a soldier on guard in the IDF need to wait to eat until he is off duty and can do so in the Sukkah?</u> No. He can eat on guard out of the Sukkah.

M. Store owners:

- People that work in stores remain obligated to eat and dwell in a Sukkah, and hence are to build a Sukkah near their store and it is forbidden to eat in the store. If they are unable to build a Sukkah near the store, they must return to the Sukkah near their home to eat there.

Chapter 2: The Laws of Daled Minim

1. The general laws:
A. The Mitzvah:
- It is a Biblical command to shake the Daled Minim [i.e. four species, or commonly summed up as "Lulav"] on the first day of Sukkos, which is the 15th of the month of Tishrei. It is a Rabbinical command to shake the Lulav throughout all seven days of the festival.
- <u>Shabbos</u>: One does not shake the Lulav on Shabbos. This applies even if the first day of Sukkos fell on Shabbos.
- <u>Shemini Atzeres</u>: The last day of shaking Lulav is on Hoshana Raba. It is not shaken on Shemini Atzeres even in the Diaspora.
- <u>Shaking in Jerusalem-old city</u>: Some Poskim rule that according to some Rishonim the shaking of Daled Minim in the old city of Jerusalem is a Biblical obligation for all seven days of the festival. Due to this, he concludes that one who shakes in the old city of Jerusalem should have intent to fulfill a command which is questionable whether it is Biblical or Rabbinical. Likewise, one should be particular to comply to all restrictions that apply to the Daled Minim on the first day of Sukkos when the shaking is Biblical. Hence, one is to use a set of Daled Minim that he owns, or receive it as a "Matana Al Menas Lehachzir". Likewise, the Daled Minim are to fulfill the validation criteria required for the first day, such as Chasar and the like. Other Poskim argue that there is no difference between the old city of Jerusalem and other areas.
- <u>Sparks of Chassidus</u>: See Shaar Hachassidus!

B. The blessing:
- A blessing is recited over the Lulav on each day that it is Shaken, including on the second day and Chol Hamoed. The wording of the blessing is "Baruch Ata…Elokeinu..Asher Kidishanu…Al Netilas Lulav."
- <u>Shehechiyanu</u>: On the first day of Sukkos [or the first time that one is shaking Lulav] one recites the blessing of Shehechiyanu. One does not say Shehechiyanu on the second day or any subsequent day. If the first day of Sukkos fell on Shabbos [and hence the Lulav will be shaken for the first time on Sunday], then Shehechiyanu is recited on the second day [i.e. Sunday].
- <u>Shaking the Daled Minim non-simultaneously</u>: If one shakes the four species non-simultaneously, but rather one after the other, he fulfills his obligation if all four species were eventually taken. All four species, however, must be present before him [or near him] at the time [of saying the blessing, in order so an interval is not made between the blessing and the shaking of all four species]. In such a case, one is to first take the Lulav and say the blessing over it [of Al Netilas Lulav] and intend to include the shaking of the other species [upon saying the blessing]. If one talked in-between then it is disputed amongst Poskim as to whether the blessing is to be repeated on each individual species [i.e. Al Netilas Aravah, Al Netilas Hadas, Al Netilas Esrog]. [Practically, it is best for the blessing not to be repeated, although one is to say the blessings in his mind. Nevertheless, one who repeats the blessing has upon whom to rely.]
- <u>If after the shaking one discovered an invalidation in the four species, is a blessing repeated?</u> If after shaking the Daled Minim one realized that one of them was invalid, such as the

Hadas or Aravah was missing or had no leaves or was upside down, he must re-shake a Kosher species of the invalidated or missing species. From the letter of the law, he has fulfilled his obligation of all the Kosher species that he took, and is thus not required to re-shake all four species together, but rather simply the invalidated or missing species alone. Nonetheless, it is a Mitzvah Min Hamuvchar to re-shake all four species together. Regarding the blessing: It is disputed amongst Poskim as to whether the blessing is to be repeated on the species. [Practically, Safek Brachos Lihakel and a blessing is not to be repeated, although one who does so has upon whom to rely.]

- If one picked up the Lulav and Esrog prior to saying the blessing, may a blessing still be recited? If one did not yet shake the Lulav, then one may say the blessing prior to shaking the Lulav. If one already shook the Lulav but did not yet Daven Hallel, see next!

- If one accidently shook the Lulav without a blessing, may a blessing still be recited? If one lifted and shook the Lulav without a blessing then some Poskim rule a blessing may no longer be recited, even if one did not yet recite Hallel. This applies even if the Lulav and Esrog are still in one's hands. Other Poskim, however, rule that if one has not yet Davened Hallel, a blessing may be recited prior to Hallel. Furthermore, some Poskim rule even after Hallel a blessing may be recited if one did not perform Hoshanos. If, however, one already recited Hoshanos, the blessing may not be recited even according to this latter opinion.

- If one shook the Lulav without reciting Shehechiyanu on the first day, what is he to do? This follows the same law as above regarding one who shook the Lulav without a blessing, that if he is prior to Hallel, or even prior to Hoshanos, then some Poskim rule the blessing may still be recited. In the event that the blessing may no longer be recited, it is to be said the next day.

- If one is shaking Lulav for the second time that day, using another person Lulav, is a new blessing to be recited? No.

C. Women shaking Lulav:
- Women are exempt from the Mitzvah of shaking Lulav. Nevertheless, if they desire to shake Lulav, they may do so. Practically, women have accepted upon themselves the Mitzvah shaking of Lulav as an obligation. [Accordingly, women are to be particular to shake Lulav each day of Sukkos, due to the accepted custom. It is likewise customary to educate girls to shake Lulav.]

- The blessing: A woman [of Ashkenazi origin] who shakes Lulav, may choose to recite a blessing prior to doing so, just as a man recites prior to performing the Mitzvah. [On the first day, or by her first time, she may likewise recite the blessing of Shehechiyanu.] If, however, a woman does not know how to say the blessing, a man may not say the blessing on her behalf. [A blessing may only be recited if the Lulav set is Kosher according to Halacha, and therefore, it is imperative for women who are shaking with a blessing to be aware of the laws involved that can invalidate a Lulav set. On the first day of Sukkos, if a woman is shaking another's Lulav, it is to be given to her as a Matana Al Menas Lehachzir, just as is the rule by a man.]

- Are women to shake the Lulav in all the six directions, as is done by men? Some Poskim write that according to Kabala women are not to shake the Lulav in all the directions, but are simply to shake it one time, and it suffices.

- May a man give a woman Daled Minim to shake? Yes. Some however write one is to avoid doing so to reasons of Tznius. See next regarding a married woman.

- May one give a married woman Daled Minim to shake on the first day(s) of Sukkos? Some Poskim rule that one may not give a married woman Daled Minim to shake on the first day(s) of Sukkos unless he explicitly states that it is a Matana Al Menas Lehachzir, and the husband has no portion in it, and he is giving it to her specifically to fulfill the Mitzvah. Accordingly, on the first day of Sukkos, a married woman should be particular to shake her husband's Lulav.
- May women eat prior to shaking Lulav? It is customary for women not to eat at all until they shake Lulav. From the letter of the law women are allowed to eat up to 55 grams of Mezonos, unlimited amount of fruit and vegetables, and unlimited amounts of beverages. This certainly applies to a woman who is pregnant, nursing or feels weak. However, she should not eat a full meal or over 55 grams of Mezonos until she shakes Lulav. If, however, they feel that they require this amount of food to eat then it is completely allowed.

D. Children:
- Children which have reached the age of Chinuch are obligated to be educated in the Mitzvah of Lulav. The age of Chinuch is from when the child knows how to shake the Lulav properly [in all its directions]. The father is obligated to purchase a Lulav set for a child of this age. [Alternatively, on the first day of Sukkos, the father is to give his son the Lulav after the adults have fulfilled their obligation. Nevertheless, it is best to purchase the child his own personal set in order so he can use the Lulav during Hallel.]

E. Purchasing a set of Lulav and Esrog:
- When to buy a set of Lulav and Esrog: Some write that one is to try to purchase a set of Daled Minim during Aseres Yimei Teshuvah in order to add in merits for the day of Yom Kippur and have these merits overturn the judgment. Others however write that one is specifically to buy the Esrog after Yom Kippur as the tears of Yom Kippur clean the blemishes of the Esrog.
- Paying for the species after the holiday: One does not need to pay for the four species before Sukkos.
- Every person is to have his own set of Daled Minim: Every person is to have his own set of Daled Minim. Charity organizations are to ensure that every person can have his own set of Daled Minim and be able to build their own Sukkah.
- Buying Daled Minim for one's children: One is required to buy a set of Kosher Daled Minim on behalf of his children.
- May one buy Daled Minim from a child? One may not purchase any of the Daled Minim for adult use on the first day of Sukkos [in Eretz Yisrael, and the first two days of Sukkos in the Diaspora] from a child who is under Bar/Bas Mitzvah, if the child personally owns the Daled Minim. If one already shook Daled Minim that was purchased from a Katan, then on the first day of Sukkos [and second day in Diaspora], one is to shake it again without a blessing.
- According to all opinions, one may purchase Daled Minim from a child of any age for the sake of using them on Chol Hamoed. Thus, one may purchase extra sets of Aravos from children to use on Chol Hamoed.
- The above limitation regarding the first days of Sukkos is only in a case that the child is the actual owner of the Daled Minim, such as he picked it from Hefker, received it as a present, or purchased it with his money. If, however, the child does not own the Daled Minim and is

simply selling them on behalf of an adult, then one may even initially purchase it from a child of any age.

F. Binding the Lulav:

- The Mitzvah: The Daled Minim are initially to be shaken simultaneously. Furthermore, it is a Mitzvah Min Hamuvchar to bind the Lulav with the Hadas and Aravah in a single bind. If one shakes the four species non-simultaneously, but rather one after the other, he fulfills his obligation if all four species were eventually taken. See Halacha B for the full details of this matter!

- When: The custom is to bind the Lulav on Erev Sukkos inside the Sukkah. [The Rebbe would do so after midday.]

- Who: Those who are meticulous, make sure to personally bind the Lulav. Women and children are not to initially bind a man's Lulav.

- The material used to tie: All materials are valid for use to tie the Lulav. However, the widespread custom is to use Lulav leaves. Many make Lulav pockets out of the leaves. The Chabad custom is not to use the Lulav pockets. If one is unable to find or use Lulav leaves, he can use the branch of an Aravah to tie the Lulav. If this too is not available, any string, or rubber band, may be used.

- How to bind the Lulav:
  1. One first makes two knots on the Lulav itself using Lulav leaves.
  2. One then places a Hadas on the right, left and center of the Lulav, and places the Aravos in between in an inconspicuous fashion.
  3. The Hadassim should cover over the 2 knots on the Lulav.
  4. It is proper to bind the Hadassim and Aravos towards the bottom of the Lulav in order to also hold on to them when doing the Mitzvah. If one did not do so, he has nevertheless fulfilled the Mitzvah.
  5. One then binds three knots onto the Hadassim and Aravos. All three should be within the space 1 handbreadth (8 centimeters).
  6. Having the spine of the Lulav extend above the Hadassim and Aravos: The spine of the Lulav must reach at least one Tefach above the Hadassim/Aravos of the Lulav. The top of the spine is defined as the area from where it begins to split into two or more leaves. One must be very careful in this matter.

- Making rings and tying the Lulav on Yom Tov: It is forbidden to tie the Lulav on Yom Tov using a forbidden form of knot. Thus, one may not make a double knot, or a bow on top of a knot. Rather, one is to make a bow over a bow. [It is forbidden to do many modifications to the Lulav leaves for the sake of turning them into a knot or Lulav pocket.]

- May one remove leaves from the Lulav on Yom Tov? Some Poskim rule it is permitted to remove leaves from the Lulav on Yom Tov for the purpose of tying the Lulav on Yom Tov. Other Poskim rule it is forbidden to remove the leaves from the Lulav. Practically, in a time of need that no other binding material is available [including precut strings, rubber bands, extra Aravah branches etc.], one may be lenient to do so discreetly using a Shinuiy, such as using one's teeth and the like. According to all opinions, it is forbidden to mend and sharpen the Lulav leaves after they are plucked.

F. How to Bentch Lulav:

- <u>All four species together versus one at a time</u>: It is [initially required and] a Mitzvah Min Hamuvchar for [the Daled Minim to be shaken simultaneously and] for the Lulav, Hadas and Aravah to be bound together in a single bind during the shaking. If one shakes the four species non-simultaneously, but rather one after the other, he fulfills his obligation if all four species were eventually taken. All four species, however, must be present before him [or near him] at the time [of saying the blessing, in order so an interval is not made between the blessing and the shaking of all four species]. In such a case, one is to first take the Lulav and say the blessing over it [of Al Netilas Lulav] and intend to include the shaking of the other species [upon saying the blessing]. If one talked in-between, then it is disputed amongst Poskim as to whether the blessing is to be repeated on each individual species, as explained in Halacha B-see there!

- <u>When</u>: One is to awaken early in the morning to perform the Mitzvah of Daled Minim, especially on the first day of Sukkos. One may begin shaking Lulav from sunrise. If one is traveling, he may shake Lulav starting from after Alos. From the letter of the law, one is to fulfill the Mitzvah of shaking Lulav before Hallel. However, since it is a Mitzvah Min Hamuvchar to shake the Lulav in the Sukkah, and one cannot leave the Shul in the interim due to the onlookers, therefore in the morning prior to prayer one is to say the blessing over the Lulav in the Sukkah.

- <u>Eating prior to shaking</u>: It is forbidden to eat before shaking the Lulav. If, however, one will not be able to shake until after midday he should eat beforehand.

- May women eat prior to shaking Lulav? It is customary for women not to eat at all until they shake Lulav. From the letter of the law women are allowed to eat up to 55 grams of Mezonos, unlimited amount of fruit and vegetables, and unlimited amounts of beverages. This certainly applies to a woman who is pregnant, nursing or feels weak. However, she should not eat a full meal or over 55 grams of Mezonos until she shakes Lulav. If, however, they feel that they require this amount of food to eat then it is completely allowed.

- <u>Where</u>: One is to shake the Lulav inside the Sukkah.

G. How to hold it:

- <u>Top side facing up</u>: Each of the four species needs to be held in the order that they were grown. This means that their head/top part is to be facing up and their root/bottom part facing down. If one held the species upside down at the time that he intended to fulfill the Mitzvah, he does not fulfill his obligation with this shaking. The Pitum is considered the top part of the Esrog and the Esrog is thus to be held with its Pitum facing up.

- One must be especially careful with Hadassim that come in a bundle from far, in which case at times some of the branches are with their heads facing up while the branches are near them with their heads facing down, as well as at times they bend the head of the Hadas. Hence one is to be careful to open the bundle and verify that the Hadassim are positioned properly.

- <u>In two hands</u>: The Mitzvah of Daled Minim is for each and every Jew to take all four species the Esrog in one hand, and in the second hand to take the Lulav, Hadassim and Aravos. If one held all the Daled in one hand, it is disputed as to whether he has fulfilled the obligation. Practically, one is to re-shake the Daled Minim, with the Esrog in one hand and the Lulav and other Minim in the other hand, without a blessing.

- <u>Which hand to hold the Lulav/Esrog</u>: [A right-handed person] must hold the Lulav and its species [i.e. the Hadas and Aravah] in his right hand and the Esrog in his left hand. This applies every time he shakes the Lulav for the sake of the Mitzvah, such as by [Hallel and] Hoshanos. If one held the species in the opposite hand [i.e. Esrog in right and Lulav with species in left] he nevertheless fulfills his obligation. Nevertheless, it is proper for him to shake the Lulav a second time without a blessing.

- Lefty: One who is left-handed is to hold the Lulav in his left hand and the Esrog in his right hand. [If he held the species in the opposite hand [i.e. Esrog in left and Lulav with species in right], he nevertheless fulfills his obligation.]

- Ambidextrous: One who makes use of both his right and left hand [equally] is to take the Lulav in his right hand and the Esrog in his left hand. [If one writes with his right hand and does the remainder of his actions with his left hand, he is to hold the Lulav in his left hand. If, however, he is also able to do all his work also with his right hand, even though it is less comfortable, he is to take it in his right hand which he uses to write.]

- Chatzitza: It is forbidden to have any intervening substance between one's hands and the Lulav or Esrog or other Minim. If there was an intervening substance between one's hands and the Daled Minim, he does not fulfill his obligation. Thus, one may not shake Lulav wearing a glove.

H. The blessing process:

1. One faces east [not specifically towards Jerusalem] throughout the blessing and shaking process.
2. One takes hold of the Lulav in his right hand [if he's right-handed, as explained above].
3. The spine of the Lulav faces the person.
4. The Esrog remains on the table and is not lifted until after the blessing. One then says the Bracha of Al Netilas Lulav and lifts the Esrog in his left hand [if he is right-handed as explained above. A lefty lifts the Esrog in his right hand]. On the first day of Sukkos one now says [after lifting the Esrog] the blessing of Shehechiyanu.
5. One then adjoins the top third of the Esrog [thus having the Esrog in a slightly slanted position] with the Lulav/Hadassim and Aravos. Throughout the shaking one remains holding the Lulav in his right hand and the Esrog in his left hand [for one who is right-handed].
6. One then shakes the Lulav with the adjoined Esrog three times in six different directions. One first shakes three times southeast [towards one's right], then three times northeast [towards one's left], then three times east [frontwards], three times up, three times down, and three times west.
7. When shaking towards west, the first two times one shakes to southwest [towards one's back on his right side] and then shakes it completely towards west.
8. Throughout the shaking, the Esrog remains covered by one's hand, until the last shake where one reveals the Esrog slightly.
9. The Lulav remains facing upwards throughout all of the shakings. It is not to be turned upside down when one shakes it downwards.
10. The Lulav is to be shaken after each Holacha, prior to the Hovah.

I. Caretaking of the Daled Minim:

- <u>Watering the Lulav, Hadassim and Aravos:</u> It is a Mitzvah to keep the Lulav, Hadassim and Aravos fresh and good looking. One is to do so by placing them in a vase of water. It is a Mitzvah to change the waters during Chol Hamoed in order to ensure their freshness.
- <u>Watering the Lulav, Hadassim, Aravos on Yom Tov:</u> If water was placed into A vase or bucket from before Yom Tov, then the Lulav and Hadassim/Aravos may be entered into the bucket or vase of water on Yom Tov. It is however forbidden to initially place water in a vase or bucket on Yom Tov for the purpose of placing the Lulav, Hadassim or Aravos in it. However, it is permitted to add water to a vase on Yom Tov if it already contained water from before Yom Tov [if the amount will not exceed the original amount of water in the vase]. It is forbidden to switch the waters of the vase/bucket in all cases, even on Yom Tov.
- <u>May one sprinkle water onto his Lulav, Hadassim, Aravos on Shabbos or Yom Tov?</u> It is forbidden to do so on Shabbos. Regarding Yom Tov, some Poskim write that it is permitted to do so. Practically, it is best to avoid doing so.
- <u>Replacing the Hadassim and Aravos on Chol Hamoed:</u> One should replace the Hadassim and Aravos as the days go on in accordance to need. [We are however not particular to switch the Aravos daily, as is the custom of others.]
- <u>How to replace the Hadassim and Aravos:</u> One is not to stick the new Hadassim and Aravos into the knot that is over the Lulav. This causes leaves to shear and can invalidate the branch, as well as invalidate the status of the knot. Rather one is to undo the knots and then place the new Hadassim/Aravos, and then retie them together.

J. Smelling the Esrog and Hadassim during Sukkos:

- One may not smell the Hadassim throughout Sukkos.
- One is to avoid smelling the Esrog even on Shabbos.

K. The Daled Minim on Yom Tov:

- <u>Wrapping the Esrog in new material:</u> It is forbidden to place an Esrog on top of a cloth on Shabbos/Yom Tov due to the prohibition of Molid Reiach. This however only applies if one intends to create a new smell on the garment, while if one does not intend to create a new smell, then doing so is permitted.
- <u>On Yom Tov may one carry his Daled Minim back home after having used it for the Mitzvah?</u> [It is forbidden for one to carry on Yom Tov in an area without an Eiruv for a non-Yom Tov need.] Thus, it is forbidden to carry the Daled Minim in a Reshus Harabim [i.e. public domain] for no Halachic need of that day. [This prohibition includes even carrying the Daled Minim through a Karmalis that does not contain an Eiruv. It is however permitted to carry it in any city that contains an Eiruv that permits carrying on Shabbos, even if one is carrying it for no need at all. Likewise, one may carry it in a courtyard from one house to another, or from one courtyard to another even if Eiruv Chatzeiros was not performed.]
- <u>May one carry a set of Daled Minim on behalf of women?</u> It is permitted to carry the Daled Minim through a public domain for the sake of women shaking Lulav.
- <u>May one carry the Daled Minim back home after concluding the Mitzvah?</u> If one originally carried the Daled Minim to Shul on Yom Tov, then if he suspects the Lulav may get lost or stolen if he leaves it in Shul, he may return it home on Yom Tov even if he has no more need to shake it that day. If, however one brought the Daled Minim to Shul from <u>before</u> Yom Tov then he may not carry it back home on Yom Tov unless he needs to use it there for the

Mitzvah. [This applies even if one suspects the Daled Minim may get stolen if one leaves it in Shul. If, however one has a safe area to leave the Daled Minim in Shul, such as a locker, then he may not carry it back home even if he brought it there on Yom Tov, unless he plans to use it at home. If one carried the Daled Minim from Shul for the sake of Mivtzaim he may return it back home even if it was brought to Shul before Yom Tov.]

L. The Daled Minim on Shabbos:

- Is an Esrog Muktzah on Shabbos? An Esrog designated as merchandise: If the owner is particular to not use it for any purpose [such as not even to smell] then they are Muktzah Machmas Chisaron Kis. An Esrog of personal use: Esrogim which one has bought for personal use are not Muktzah on Shabbos, as they are fit to be smelled. This applies likewise on Shabbos Chol Hamoed, as although they may not be smelled during Sukkos, including Shabbos Chol Hamoed, nevertheless they are not Muktzah.

- Hadassim: Hadassim of personal use are not Muktzah on the Shabbosim prior to Sukkos, although they are Muktzah on Shabbos Chol Hamoed.

- Lulav/Aravos: Is always Muktzah on Shabbos, whether of merchandise or personal use, whether Shabbos Chol Hamoed or other Shabbosim.

2. General Kashrus laws of the Daled Minim

- Showing the species to a Rav: Due to the vast amount of Halachos involved in the Kashrus of the four species it is strongly recommended that one show them to a Rav to make sure it fulfills the Halachic requirements, and to verify what level of *hiddur* it has. Due to differences in Halachic opinions, those faithful to the Alter Rebbe's Shulchan Aruch should have them viewed by a Rav who rules in accordance with the Alter Rebbe.

A. Taking all four species:

- The Mitzvah of Daled Minim is for each and every Jew to take all four species; the Esrog, Lulav, Hadassim and Aravos. All four species are required to be taken [and be Kosher] in order to fulfill the Mitzvah. If one of the species is missing, one cannot take another species in its place. In such a case [that a species is missing], a blessing is not to be said on the other species that are available. Nonetheless, one is to take the available species without a blessing for commemoration purposes. This applies on all days of Sukkos, both the first day and the remaining days. However, one is never to take a different species in exchange for one of the four species, [even for commemoration purposes]. The next Halacha will discuss the amount of each species that must be taken, and if one may take more than required.
- Taking more than four Minim: It is [Biblically] forbidden to add another species [i.e. a rosemary branch] to the four species [upon shaking the four species for the Mitzvah] due to the prohibition of Baal Tosif. [This, however, only applies if one takes the additional species with intent to join it in fulfillment of the Mitzvah. If, however, it just happens to be in one's hand, one does not Biblically transgress Baal Tosif. Nonetheless, initially one is not to do so being that it appears as if one is adding to the Mitzvah. Additionally, this may pose a Chatzitza/interval invalidation, as explained in Chapter 2 Halacha G.]

B. How many of each species is one to take?

- Lulav: One takes one Lulav. It is forbidden to take more than one Lulav.
- Esrog: One takes one Esrog. It is forbidden to take more than one Esrog.
- Hadassim: One takes three Hadassim branches. In a time of need in which one cannot find three Hadassim, one fulfills his obligation with even one Hadas branch.
- It is permitted to take more than three Hadassim, and one may take whatever amount one wishes. Nevertheless, those who are particular, do not take more than three Hadassim. [Practically, the Chabad custom is to take more than three Hadassim. Various people have been instructed by the Chabad Rabbeim to take 4, 12, 13, or 26 Hadassim, but not 9, 68, or 69. One should try at the very least to add at least 3 more Hadassim to the minimal three required.]
- Some Poskim rule that it is forbidden to add an invalid Hadas to the Lulav [even if it is] in addition to the three Kosher Hadassim. Other Poskim, however, rule it is permitted to do so.
- Aravos: One takes two Aravos branches. Some Poskim rule that one does not fulfill his obligation if only one Aravah was taken [and hence he must repeat the shaking with a blessing over the Aravah]. However, other Poskim rule one is Yotzei Bedieved with even one Aravah. Practically, if one shook with only one Aravah, or only one Kosher Aravah, one is to re-shake two Aravos without a blessing. In a time of need that only one Kosher Aravah is available, one is to shake the Daled Minim without a blessing.

- It is permitted to take more than two Aravos, and one may take whatever amount one wishes. Nevertheless, those who are particular do not take more than two Aravos.

C. Owning the Daled Minim:

- Using another person's Daled Minim: On the 1st day of Sukkos [in Eretz Yisrael and the first two days of Sukkos in the Diaspora as will be explained next] one only fulfills his obligation with a set of Daled Minim which he personally owns. Therefore, when using someone else's Lulav one must receive it as a present on condition to return. Thus, the giver should explicitly say to the recipient "It is a present on condition you return it". If this was not explicitly said and rather the Daled Minim were simply given to the person without mentioning anything, he has nevertheless fulfilled his obligation. If, however the receiver did not know the law that he must own the Daled Minim then he has not fulfilled his obligation and is to be given it again as a present on condition to return.
- Second day of Sukkos in Diaspora: On the second day of Sukkos in the Diaspora one may not say a blessing over a Lulav that he does not own. Hence, he is to be given the Lulav as a present on condition to return.
- Chol Hamoed: During Chol Hamoed one does not need to use a Lulav which he owns. [Nevertheless, it is proper to give another person one's Lulav as a Matana Al Menas Lehachzir also during Chol Hamoed, and this is beneficial for both the giver and the receiver. So was the custom of the Rebbe.]
- On Chol Hamoed, one may use another person's Lulav without permission, assuming he doesn't mind. However, it is forbidden to remove the Lulav from its place unless the owner was asked.
- Returning the Daled Minim: The receiver is to return the Daled Minim to the owner as a present with intent that the owner acquires it [as opposed to lending the Daled Minim to the original owner]. If the receiver did not return the Daled Minim he has not fulfilled his obligation. This applies even if he was given the Daled Minim without having it said explicitly that it was a present on condition to return. The receiver may give the Lulav and Esrog to another person as a present on condition to fulfill his obligation and this person himself may also give it to another, as long as the original owner receives it in return, as originally stipulated.
- Joint ownership of a set of Daled Minim: If a Lulav or Esrog, or any of the Daled Minim, is under joint ownership, each owner must give his portion to his partner as a present [on condition to return] in order to fulfill his obligation.
- A stolen Lulav set: One who buys a stolen species only fulfills his obligation if the owner has given up hope in retrieving it.
- Is the shaking of Daled Minim in Jerusalem during exile a Biblical or Rabbinical obligation throughout all seven days? Some Poskim rule that according to some Rishonim the shaking of Daled Minim in the old city of Jerusalem is a Biblical obligation for all seven days of the festival. Due to this he concludes that one who shakes in the old city of Jerusalem should have intent to fulfill a command which is questionable whether it is Biblical or Rabbinical. Likewise, one should be particular to comply to all restrictions that apply to the Daled Minim on the first day of Sukkos when the shaking is Biblical. Hence one is to use a set of Daled Minim that he owns or receive it as a "Matana Al Menas Lehachzir". Likewise, the Daled Minim are to fulfill the validation criteria required for the first day, such as Chasar and the

like. Other Poskim argue that there is no difference between the old city of Jerusalem and other areas.

D. Giving it to a Katan:

- On the first day of Sukkos in Eretz Yisrael, and the first two days of Sukkos in the Diaspora, one is not to give his personal Daled Minim to any child below the age of 13 for a boy and 12 for a girl, to fulfill the Mitzvah. Thus, one must purchase a separate set of Daled Minim for the children to shake. Alternatively, on the first day in Eretz Yisrael, and on the second day in the Diaspora, one may give the child his personal Daled Minim if all the adults have already fulfilled the Mitzvah. However, on the first day in the Diaspora one is not to give children his personal Daled Minim even after all the adults have already fulfilled the Mitzvah, as one must use his own set of Lulav also the next day.

- If the child does not have his own set: If one does not have another Lulav available to give the children then he may give the children his personal Lulav as a borrowed item, and not as a present. Thus, he is not to say, "a present on condition to return", as he does when giving it to adults. Nevertheless, some Poskim rule that the child may not say a blessing on this shaking.

- If one gave the child the set as a present: If one did give the child the Daled Minim as a present then no other adults may fulfill their obligation with this Lulav until the start of Chol Hamoed. If one gave the child his Daled Minim without mentioning anything at all, and he also did not have anything in mind, then it is considered lent to the child and other adults may still fulfill their obligation with it even on the first days of Sukkos by having it given to them as a present.

- May one give the Daled Minim on first day [and second day in Diaspora] to a boy/girl above Bar or Bas Mitzvah on condition to return if they are under 18? Some Poskim rule one may not initially give the Daled Minim on the first day of Sukkos to a child even above Bar/Bas Mitzvah, if other adults still need to be Yotzei with it, and the child has not yet grown a substantial amount of facial hair, and is below age 18. Other Poskim, however, rule that it is even initially permitted to give the Daled Minim to such a child who is above Bar/Bas Mitzvah, as a Matana Al Means Lehachzir, even though he is under 18 and has not yet grown facial hair. [Practically, it is a proper to initially purchase a set of Daled Minim for such a child, or not give it to such a child so long as other adults still need to shake. However, in a time of need, one may give it to any child above Bar/Bas Mitzvah and then return and use it for other adults even with a blessing, according to all opinions.]

- May Bochurim who are above Bar Mitzvah, but below age 18, perform Mivtzaim on the first day of Sukkos using their own set of Daled Minim? Yes.

- May a child give another child his Lulav and Esrog to shake? Yes, if the child is above age 6.

- Must one give his wife the Lulav and Esrog on condition of returning? Some Poskim require one to give his wife the set of Daled Minim as a present on condition to return. Others however rule there is no need to be particular in this.

- May one give married women Daled Minim to shake on the first day(s) of Sukkos? Some Poskim rule that one may not give a married woman Daled Minim to shake on the first day(s) of Sukkos unless he explicitly states that it is a Matana Al Menas Lehachzir, and the husband has no portion in it, and he is giving it to her specifically to fulfill the Mitzvah.

E. The requirement of Hadar:

- The Torah states that the Esrog must be Hadar which means beautiful in appearance and growth. This applies likewise to all four species, as the command of all four species are written in the same verse, hence juxtaposing them together and creating a legal bridge to transfer laws from one species to another. The exact definition of Hadar will be discussed in each species.

F. The requirement of Shaleim:

- The Torah states "Ulikachtem Lachem", from which the Sages expounded that the Daled Minim must be complete and whole. The exact definition of Shaleim will be discussed in each species.

G. Cooked or soaked in water:

- A cooked Esrog is invalid for the Mitzvah. Thus, an Esrog which stayed submerged in water, or other liquids, for over 24 hours is Pasul, as it is considered cooked. It is disputed amongst the Poskim as to whether this invalidation of cooked/Kavush applies likewise to the other species, Lulav, Hadassim and Aravos, even though they are not foods. Practically, one is initially to avoid leaving any of the Daled Minim in water for 24 consecutive hours. Aravos and Hadassim that sit in buckets of water are to be removed within 24 hours, and not to be left in the water over Shabbos.

H. The Kashrus laws on Chol Hamoed:

- <u>Shaleim invalidations</u>: On Chol Hamoed, all Shaleim invalidations are Kosher. The exact details of this matter will be explained by each individual invalidation.
- <u>Hadar invalidations</u>: It is disputed if Hadar invalidations are invalid during Chol Hamoed, just like on the first day. Practically, one may not initially use on Chol Hamoed Daled Minim which contain a Hadar invalidation, however if no other Kosher species is available, then one may use it [even with a Bracha].

I. The Kashrus laws on the second day in Diaspora:

- On the second day of Sukkos in the Diaspora, a Daled Minim which contains a first day invalidation is disputed if it is invalid, just like on the first day, or retains the leniencies of Chol Hamoed [as explained above]. Practically, one is not to use such a Daled Minim, and if no other Kosher species is available, and one cannot borrow one from another person, then one is to use it without a Bracha.

J. Using non-Kosher Daled Minim in a time of need:

- Some Poskim rule that if a Kosher species is unavailable, then one may use an invalid Daled Minim with a blessing throughout all the days of Sukkos, including on the first day. This, however, is limited only to Daled Minim that contain invalidations that are due to a blemish which is readily apparent on the Daled Minim, such as lack of Shaleim or Hadar, however, if it contains other invalidations which are not due to a blemish, then it is not to be used at all even without a blessing. Other Poskim, however, argue on all the above and rule that all invalidations remain invalid, including lack of Hadar/Shaleim, even if no other Daled Minim is available, and it may never be taken with a blessing. However, if the invalidation is due to a blemish, then it may be taken without a blessing for mere commemoration. Practically, some communities follow the former approach while others follow the latter approach.

- Bedieved: The above discussion is only in a case that there is no Kosher Daled Minim available. If, however, a Kosher species is available, then one does not fulfill his obligation at all with a non-Kosher species even Bedieved, and he must re-shake the Kosher species with a blessing.

Checklist of what to look for when purchasing Daled Minim:

The following is a list of matters one is to look for to purchase a Kosher and Mehudar set of Daled Minim.

Esrog:
1. It is a Calabria Esrog from Italy.
2. Verify there are no missing pieces anywhere from the Esrog.
3. Verify it does not have a broken Pitam.
4. Verify it does not have a broken Oketz.
5. Verify the Chotem is clean of a Chazazis/blister or color change.
6. Verify that below the Chotem there is not two Chazazis or two-color changes.
7. Bletlach are Kosher.
8. Verify that has a Hashgacha if it came from Israel.
9. It is preferable that the Esrog be completely yellow.

Lulav:
1. Its spine is at least 32cm. and will extend a Tefach past Hadassim/Aravos.
2. Its Tiyomus is completely closed on its top.
3. The Tiyomus is double leafed from top to bottom.
4. Majority of the other leaves are also majority closed.
5. The Tiyomus is not cut on its top.
6. It is not bent to any side. The Lulav is straight.
7. The leaves are not bent.
8. The Tiyomus is not dry.
9. Some prefer that the Lulav contain a Kara brown covering.

Hadassim:
1. Is at least 24 cm.
2. The first 24 cm from the top is completely Meshulash, or at the very least majority Meshulash.
3. The top is not cut off.
4. Remove random leaves.

Aravos:
1. Is at least 24 cm.
2. The first 24 cm from the top has all of its leaves intact, or at the very least majority of its leaves.
3. The top is not cut off.

3. The Lulav
A. The Meaning of the Lulav:
See Shaar Hachassidus 3!

B. The identity of the Lulav:
- The Torah states that one is to take a Kapos Temarim. This refers to a branch that grows on a date palm.
- Is a male palm tree [i.e. do not grow dates] Lulav's valid? Yes. It is not necessary for the palm tree to grow dates.
- The canary palm: Some Poskim rule that the canary Lulav is invalid and it is a Bracha Levatala to say a blessing over it. Other Poskim rule it is valid even initially.
- How to identify a canary: 1. The spine of the canary palm bends when held. 2. Its leaves grow closer together. 3. It has a very short spine.

C. Length:
- Minimum length: The length of the spine of the Lulav must be four Tefach. If the Hadassim or Aravos are more than three Tefach, than the spine of the Lulav must be at least one Tefach higher than the Hadassim and Aravos.
- How much is four Tefachim? Some Poskim rule that every Tefach is 4 Agudlin and hence four Tefachim is 16 Agudlin [32cm.] Others, however, rule that each Tefach is 3.33 Tefach and hence four Tefach is 13.3 Agudlin [26.6 cm]. Practically, we are stringent to follow the first opinion of 32 cm. However, in a time of need one may be lenient to use a Lulav that has a spine of 26.6 cm. If one already used such a Lulav and then found a Lulav with 32 cm, he should shake it without a blessing being that he has already fulfilled his obligation.
- How to measure the four Tefachim: The 32 cm is measured from the bottom of the spine [in the area that a pair of leaves begin to grow on each side] until the top of the spine. The top area of the spine where the spine splits into two leaves [i.e. the Tiyomus] is not considered part of the spine, and thus one must have 32cm of spine from below this area.
- Is there a maximum length for the Lulav? No. Furthermore, some Poskim rule that that it is a Hiddur Mitzvah to have a long Lulav.]

D. How many leaves must cover the spine of the Lulav?
- The Lulav contains a spine which is covered with leaves that grow at a distance of four centimeters apart. Thus, after the first leaf grows on the spine another leaf grows 4 centimeter above it, and so on and so forth until the entire spine is covered with leaves. The leaves are on both sides of the spine, across from each other. If only one side of the spine has leaves, the Lulav is invalid. If the Lulav has only one leaf growing on each side, the Lulav is invalid. [This implies that if there are two leaves on each side it is valid.]
- The Lulav is only valid if the leaves cover each other as opposed to growing one under the other. This means if the bottom leaf does not reach the leaf above it, it is invalid. If, however, it reaches and slightly cover the leaf that is growing above it, then it is valid.

E. Must the leaves be bound together:
- It is a Mitzvah Min Hamuvchar to purchase a Lulav which its leaves have not separated at all from the spine and are thus completely bound. If the leaves began hardening and separating

from the spine, it is valid so long as the leaves are still potentially able to be bound to the spine. If majority of the leaves have separated to the point that they have hardened and can no longer be joined to the spine of the Lulav, it is invalid.

- Leaves that bend downwards: If the majority of the leaves of the Lulav do not rise together with the spine of the Lulav and rather bend downwards below the spine, then the Lulav is Biblically invalid. This applies even if one binds the leaves onto the spine using string and the like. This applies even if the leaves have not completely separated from the spine.

F. A split leaf:

- The leaves of the Lulav grow in a pair of two leaves which are parallel to each other. The two leaves are attached to each other by their back and open in their front. If majority of the leaves of the Lulav have separated in the majority of their length, the Lulav is invalid. If the majority of the leaves grew without being double paired on majority of their length, the Lulav is invalid. The same applies if majority of the leaves grew with separated pairs, it is invalid. [If, however, the leaves are double sided in majority of their length, the Lulav is valid.]

G. The law of the Tiyomus:

- What is the Tiyomus? In Halacha, special attention is given to the Tiyomus of the Lulav, and the criteria it must fulfill for the Lulav to be Kosher. The term Tiyomus comes from the word "twins," and refers to the back area of the leaf of a Lulav, where the leaves are attached as pairs, or twins. More specifically, the Poskim explain that the Tiyomus refers to the top center leaf, which is higher than all the other leaves, and extends from the spine of the Lulav. [If a Lulav has two middle leaves of equal height, some Poskim rule that both leaves have the status of a Tiyomus.] This leaf, being that it grows in the center of the Lulav and is the highest leaf, is considered the head of the Lulav. Therefore, special laws and criteria are given to this top center leaf. In this Halacha, we will discuss the law if the Tiyomus leaf split by its back, and separated from its pair.
- The law if the leaf split entirely: If the Tiyomus grew without a double-sided leaf, the Lulav is invalid on the first day(s) of Sukkos even if all the other leaves are double sided. Likewise, if the Tiyomus grew double sided and afterwards split entirely from the top until the spine, it is invalid.
- The law if the leaf partially split: Lechatchila, it is a Mitzvah Min Hamuvchar to buy a Lulav whose double leafed Tiyomus is completely attached to each other (at their back) from its top to the point the other leaves begin shooting out from the spine. If this is not available, or it split after buying it, then the Lulav remains valid so long as the leaf is not completely separated from top to bottom [where the other leaves begin growing from it]. Furthermore, even if one has a friend who owns a Lulav with a complete Tiyomus, one is not required to use it on the first day of Sukkos and rather may use his Lulav that has a partially split Tiyomus.
- Must the Tiyomus be double leafed throughout its entire length? It is implied from Admur that it is a Mitzvah Min Hamuvchar for the Tiyomus to be entirely double leafed from the top of the Tiyomus until the area of the spine, and so rule some Rabbanim. However, others learn that it is not necessary for the Tiyomus to be entirely double leafed and so is the ruling of other Rabbanim.
- What if the Tiyomus is split only at its tip as is common to occur? It is a Mitzvah Min

Hamuvchar to purchase a Tiyomus that is completely closed, including its tip.

- If the split of the Tiyomus is only noticeable after close examination is it initially invalid? Initially one is to purchase a Lulav that its Tiyomus is completely closed even after close examination. [However, it is not necessary to use a magnifying glass.]
- Gluing a split Tiyomus leaf back together? Some Poskim rule it is valid to glue the Tiyomus together.
- Hemnick split: If there is a split in the spine and the two sides of the split have separated from each other to the point they appear like two Lulavim, then the Lulav is invalid.
- On Chol Hamoed: All the above discussion of invalidation, and initial practice, regarding a split Tiyomus, only applies on the first day(s) of Sukkos, when the Mitzvah of Lulav is Biblical. However, on Chol Hamoed, a Lulav which has a deficiency of not being complete, is valid. Accordingly, during Chol Hamoed, a Lulav which contains even a completely split Tiyomus, is Kosher.
- On the second day of Sukkos in Chutz Laaretz: It is debated in Poskim as to whether the second day of Sukkos in the Diaspora Rabbinically retains the stricter laws of the first day, regarding invalidations, or if it receives the leniencies associated with Chol Hamoed regarding invalidations. Practically, Safek Brachos Lihakel, and therefore if one contains a Lulav with a completely split Tiyomus, he is to borrow another person's Lulav on the second day and recite the blessing over it. He may use his own Lulav for the Nanuim of Hallel. If there is no other Lulav available, he is to use it without a blessing.

H. A cut leaf:

- Tiyomus: Lechatchila, if the Tiyomus leaf was even partially cut at its top, the Lulav should not be used. If, however, no other Lulav is available, then if its majority length is still intact, it may be used with a blessing. If majority of the Tiyomus has been cut, it is invalid according to all opinions. [Thus, one is to avoid buying a Lulav with a very pointy top as it is easily possible for this point to break and invalidate the Lulav for initial use.]
- Remaining leaves: If the remaining leaves of a Lulav, other than the Tiyomus have been cut at their top, it remains Kosher.
- What is the law if the cut of the Tiyomus is only noticeable after close examination? Some Poskim rule that a cut Tiyomus only invalidates a Lulav if its missing area is viewable and recognizable from a fair distance to all people. If, however, one must discern with his eye in order to notice it, then it is not an invalidating missing piece, and the Lulav remains Kosher. Other Poskim, however, rule the Lulav is initially invalid if any amount of the Tiyomus is missing, even if it is a very small amount that is not discernable at first glance, and requires contemplation to be noticed, and so is implied from the Poskim.
- Many Lulavim grow a needle like wooden point at the top of the Tiyomus. If this area is cut off the Lulav remains Kosher, as this area is not considered part of the actual Lulav.

I. A dry Lulav:

- A Lulav which majority of its leaves have withered, or majority of its spine has withered, to the point it has turned whitish, should not be used unless absolutely no other Lulav is available. If it has dried to the point it can be broken by touching it with one's nail, it is Pasul according to all opinions.
- What is the law if the Tiyomus has dried? Seemingly according to Admur the Lulav remains

Kosher and Mehudar, however other Poskim rule that one should not use a Lulav with dry Tiyomus. A sunburned Tiyomus is not considered dry even according to those who are stringent.

- <u>What is the law if the dryness of the Lulav is only noticeable after close examination?</u> Some Poskim rule that it is valid, as the invalidation of Hadar is only applicable if viewable at first sight.

J. A Lulav with wrinkles:

- If the spine contains needles or if the Lulav is wrinkled it is invalid.

K. A bent Lulav/Kneplach:

- <u>Spine is bent</u>: If the spine of the Lulav is bent towards its front making it appear like a hunchback, it is not Kosher. Similarly, if it is bent to its side, it is invalid. If the middle of the spine is bent towards its back, meaning towards the side of the spine, it is Kosher. If the middle of the spine itself is straight while the top of the spine is bent like a Hegmon, the Lulav is invalid. This applies whether the Lulav is bent backwards or forwards.
- <u>Leaves are bent</u>: If majority of the leaves of a Lulav are slightly bent or curved at their top, it may not be used unless there is no other Lulav available, in which case it may be used with a blessing. If only a minority of its leaves are curved, it may be used even Lechatchila. If [majority] of the actual leaves [not just the top] are very bent in a way that each leaf appears like two leaves, the Lulav is invalid according to all.
- <u>On Chol Hamoed</u>: Even if majority of the leaves are bent or curved it is Kosher even Lechatchila.
- <u>Second day of Yom Tov in Diaspora</u>: If majority of the leaves are bent or curved one may use the Lulav if no other Lulav is easily available.
- <u>What is the law if only the Tiyomus is bent?</u> From Admur it is implied that the Lulav remains Kosher according to all opinions if majority of the leaves are not bent, even if the Tiyomus is bent. However, some Poskim are stringent.
- <u>Kneplach-Rounded tips</u>: Based on the above, the top leaves of the Lulav should not have rounded tips known as Kneplach.

L. Kura:

- Some Poskim rule that a Lulav is only valid if all its leaves are attached to each other as a single unit. This however only applies to a Lulav which originally grew with all its leaves attached and later separated, while if it initially grew separated it is valid even in their opinion. This is commonly found amongst Lulavim that grow a brownish leaf on their back, called a Kora, which attaches all the leaves together into one unit, and fulfills the requirements according to this opinion. If this leaf falls off and the leaves separate in majority of their length, then it is invalid. Other Poskim however rule that even if the brown leaf comes off and the leaves separate it remains valid, so long as the Tiyomus has not fully separated. The final ruling follows the latter opinion.]
- Practically, some are particular to purchase a Lulav with the brownish leaf covering. Others are particular not to purchase such a Lulav. The Rebbe was particular to purchase a Lulav which its top leaves are attached with a brownish leaf called a Kara.

4. The Esrog:

A. The species:

- The verse states one is to take a "Peri Eitz Hadar". The Sages deduced from the superfluous word "tree" that the fruit referred to in the verse contains a tree bark that has the same taste as its fruit, and this is an Esrog, as its tree and fruit have the same taste. [This means that the peel of the Esrog which makes up majority of the Esrog tastes similar to the bark of the tree, however the juice that it contains is not similar in taste to the bark.]

- The spiritual meaning of the Esrog: The Esrog contains a certain aspect of unity which differs from all other fruits in the world. All fruits have a season of growth during the year, while the Esrog remains on the tree for the entire year, throughout all four seasons. Thus, the Esrog fruit unifies all the seasons of the year. The Midrash explains that the Esrog represents the people who spend their time performing Mitzvos and Gemilus Chassadim as well as learning Torah. Torah and Mitzvos correspond to the good taste and good smell found in the Esrog.

B. Dryness:

- An Esrog which dried to the point it has lost all of its inside moisture is invalid. This means that the Esrog does not release moisture when cut. There is no obligation to inspect an Esrog which appears fresh. If, however, the Esrog appears withered, it must be checked.

- Is an Esrog from the previous year valid? An Esrog from the previous year is certain to have dried to the point of invalidation and therefore may not be used.

- If one froze or refrigerated an Esrog from the previous year and it appears fresh, may it be used? Some Poskim rule the Esrog is permitted to be used if it appears fresh. However, other Poskim rule the Esrog is invalid even if it appears fresh as it is common for the Esrog to completely spoil after a few days of being outside of its preservation.

C. An Esrog with a hole or missing piece:

- Hole, but no missing piece: If there is a hole in the Esrog without any piece of the Esrog missing, such as a hole that was created by sticking a large needle into the Esrog, then if the hole does not reach the seed box, or go from side to side, and is smaller than an Issur, the Esrog remains even initially valid. If it reaches seed box, or goes side to side, or is size of an Issur then it is only valid with a blessing if no other Esrog available.

- Missing piece-1st day of Yom Tov: An Esrog which is missing any part from its body, even the smallest amount, is Pasul. This applies even if the hole does not reach from one to the other and is not the size of an Issur. However, there are opinions who rule that even a hole with a missing piece is valid if it is not larger than an Issur and does not go from side to side. Practically, one may rely on this opinion if there is no other Esrog available, and one may use it with a blessing. If the missing piece is as large as the circumference of an Issur coin, it is Pasul according to all opinions.

- How small of a missing piece invalidates an Esrog? Some Poskim rule that a missing piece only invalidates an Esrog if its missing area is viewable and recognizable from a fair distance to all people. If, however, one must discern with his eye in order to notice it, then it is not an invalidating missing piece, and the Esrog remains Kosher. Other Poskim, however, rule the Esrog is invalid if any amount is missing, even if it is a very small amount that is not discernable at first glance, and requires contemplation to be noticed, and so is implied from the Poskim.

- <u>Checking with a magnifying glass if a piece is missing</u>: According to all opinions, a missing piece that is unnoticeable to the naked eye and can only be seen through a magnifying glass, does not invalidate the Esrog.
- <u>Doubt</u>: If one is in doubt whether a piece is missing from the Esrog or if it is just an indentation, the Esrog is permitted [so long as the hole is not the size of an Issur and is not Mefulash from one side to the other, or to the seed box].
- <u>The missing piece has changed color</u>: If a change of color, from its natural born color, occurred in the missing area of the Esrog, see Halacha F!
- <u>A piece missing from the outer membrane</u>: The above invalidation only applies if there is a piece missing from the actual body [white thick peel] of the Esrog. If, however, the Esrog is only missing part of its thin outer membrane [i.e. skin/rind] and its inner white thick peel remains complete, the Esrog is Kosher. If, however, the entire outer peel is missing the Esrog is invalid.
- If the missing outer membrane has caused a change in color which differs from the color of the rest of the Esrog, it receives the same Halachic status as a blister, and hence the Esrog is invalid unless the color change is not within the Chotem of the Esrog and is not majority of the Esrog and it is not within 2-3 areas of the Esrog.
- If the green external peel of the Esrog has been removed, thus revealing the white underlying peel, but without removing any part of it, is the Esrog still valid? Some Poskim rule that although the Esrog is not considered to be missing any piece, [and is thus not invalid due to Chaser, as explained above], nevertheless, it is viewed as containing a color change, and follows all of its invalidating rules. Other Poskim rule that the white rind of the Esrog is a natural color, and is not defined as a color change.
- <u>Scars and scabs</u>: A hole which was caused by a thorn while the Esrog was still on the tree, is Kosher even if a piece of the Esrog is missing as a result of the prick, if the entire area of the hole is covered by scar tissue. This applies even if there remains piece visibly missing from the Esrog, being that the missing area is fully covered by the scab. If, however, the scab is not fully covering over the hole, or there is no scab at all, and one can tell that there is a piece missing, the Esrog is invalid.
- <u>Yom Tov Sheiyni Shel Galuyos</u>: On the second day of Sukkos in the Diaspora, if an Esrog is missing a piece the size of an Issur coin one may use it if no other Esrog is available, but <u>without</u> a Bracha. If the hole is less than the size of an Issur, it may be used with a blessing if no other Esrog is available, as ruled regarding the first day.
- <u>On Chol Hamoed</u>: On Chol Hamoed an Esrog is Kosher even if it is missing a piece, and even if the missing piece is much larger than an Issur coin, so long as the Esrog retains its minimum size.

D. A cracked Esrog:
- <u>Crack in the length</u>: An Esrog which contains a crack is only invalid if the following conditions are met: 1) The crack reaches from the top of the Esrog to the bottom of the Esrog. 2) The depth of the crack reaches into majority of the thickness of the white flesh of the Esrog. If the crack is not this deep throughout its entire length, but rather only in its middle, while the top and bottom of the crack is not this deep, then the Esrog is Kosher.
- <u>Crack in width</u>: If there is a crack along the circumference of the Esrog, then if there are two cracks, one on each side of the Esrog, parallel to each other, then if there remains an un-cracked area between the two cracks, the Esrog is valid. This applies even if the depth of the

crack reaches into majority of the width of the white thick peel of the Esrog. [If, however, a single crack carries through majority of the circumference, it is implied from Admur that the Esrog is invalid.]

E. Blisters:

- An Esrog must look beautiful, otherwise known as Hadar. This is not just a subjective form of beauty, but a beauty that carries Halachic definition and invalidations. Due to the obligation of Hadar, an Esrog which contains blisters is potentially invalid, depending on the form of the blister, its size and its location on the Esrog.

- What is a Chazazis? A Chazazis is a scab like protuberance made up of two small blisters. If it only has one blister, it is not considered a Chazazis and is valid even if the blister is on the Chotem.

- Apparent at first sight: A Chazazis is only problematic if it is casually noticeable when held in one's hand without deep concentration. One is not required to contemplate and search for blisters [and if he does not see it with a regular look then the Chazazis is valid even if it is on the Chotem].

- The law on the First day of Sukkos: If there is any Halachically defined blisters in the top area of the Esrog, called the Chotem, then the Esrog is Pasul. The Chotem is defined as the area [on the upper half of the Esrog, towards the Pitam] from the point that it begins to slope inwards towards its top and becomes narrow and gradient. [See illustration below]

- If there is a Chazazis below the Chotem, then if there is only one Chazazis, the Esrog remains Kosher so long as the Chazazis does not cover majority of the Esrog. If there are two or more Chazazis, then it is disputed as to whether the Esrog remains Kosher under certain circumstances, or is always invalid, and initially one should be stringent like the latter approach to not use such an Esrog even if the two blisters are near each other. If, however, the two Chazazis are so close to each other that there is no room for another Chazazis to grow between them it is considered like one Chazazis. Likewise, if between the two Chazazisim there isn't the natural color of the Esrog, it is all considered one Chazazis. In a time of need that no other Esrog can be found, one may use an Esrog that contains two blisters below the Chotem, if from the beginning of the first blister until the end of the second color change it only covers minority of the circumference of the Esrog's width or length, such as if the two blisters are on the same side of the Esrog. If, however, it covers majority of the circumference of the Esrog's width or length, such as if the two blisters are on different sides of the Esrog, then it is Pasul according to all opinions.

- Second day in Diaspora: On the second day of Sukkos in the Diaspora, an Esrog with an invalid blister is disputed if it is invalid, just like on the first day, or retains the leniencies of Chol Hamoed [as explained next]. Practically, one is not to use such an Esrog, and if no other Esrog is available, and one cannot borrow an Esrog from another person, then one is to use it without a Bracha.

- On Chol Hamoed: The law on Chol Hamoed: During Chol Hamoed, an Esrog with an invalid blister is disputed if it is invalid, just like on the first day. Practically, one may not initially use an Esrog with an invalid blister even during Chol Hamoed, however if no other Esrog is available, then one may use such an Esrog [even with a Bracha].

- Koshering an Esrog-Peeling off the blister: An Esrog that contains an invalidating blister may be validated/Koshered through peeling off the blister from the Esrog. This is permitted to be done even initially. This applies even if the Esrog contains many blisters. The following conditions, however, must be met for it to be considered Kosher through peeling off the blister: One is to peel off only the external thin green skin of the Esrog in a way that the white body of the Esrog does not become revealed, thus assuring that nothing is missing from the body of the Esrog. [If the white skin of the Esrog becomes revealed, then it is invalid due to Chaser and possibly also due to Menumar.] After the invalidating blister is peeled off, the color of the peeled area must be similar to the color of the rest of the Esrog for it to be Kosher.

- May one peel off a blister on Yom Tov? It is forbidden to peel a blister, or any other matter, off the Esrog on Yom Tov.

F. Color Changes/spots:
- An Esrog must look beautiful, otherwise known as Hadar. This is not just a subjective form of beauty, but a beauty that carries Halachic definition and invalidations. Due to the obligation of Hadar, an Esrog must be a single solid color and may not contain spots, and certainly shades, of other colors. This Halacha will discuss the details regarding color changes and spots found on an Esrog, what is its definition, and when does it invalidate.
- The law on the First day of Sukkos: If there is any Halachically defined color change in the top area of the Esrog, called the Chotem, then the Esrog is Pasul. This applies even if the color change is a very small amount [i.e. a small black dot]. The Chotem is defined as the area [on the upper half of the Esrog, towards the Pitam] from the point that it begins to slope inwards towards its top and becomes narrow and gradient. [See illustration below]
- If there is a color change below the Chotem, then if there is only a single color change [i.e. one black dot or one white dot], the Esrog remains Kosher so long as this color does not cover majority of the Esrog. If there are two or more color changes, then it is disputed as to whether it remains Kosher under certain circumstances, or is always invalid, and initially one should be stringent like the latter approach to not use such an Esrog even if the two color changes are near each other. However, in a time of need that no other Esrog can be found, one may use an Esrog that contains two color changes below the Chotem, if from the beginning of the first color change until the end of the second color change it only covers minority of the circumference of the Esrog's width or length, such as if the two spots are on the same side of the Esrog. If, however, it covers majority of the circumference of the Esrogs width or length, such as if the two spots are on different sides of the Esrog, then it is Pasul according to all opinions.
- The law on the second day in Diaspora: On the second day of Sukkos in the Diaspora, an Esrog with an invalid color change is disputed if it is invalid, just like on the first day, or retains the leniencies of Chol Hamoed [as explained next]. Practically, one is not to use such an Esrog, and if no other Esrog is available, and one cannot borrow an Esrog from another person, then one is to use it without a Bracha.
- The law on Chol Hamoed: During Chol Hamoed, an Esrog with an invalid color change is disputed if it is invalid, just like on the first day. Practically, one may not initially use an Esrog with an invalid color change even during Chol Hamoed, however if no other Esrog is available, then one may use such an Esrog [even with a Bracha].
- The definition of a color change according to Halacha: Admur records various types of color changes:
  1. If a change of color occurred after the outer skin or rind of the Esrog was removed, the color change is viewed as potentially invalidating [depending on where it is

found, or as to in how many places]. This applies even if the color change is to a valid color that is commonly found on an Esrog.

2. A natural born color change in one area.
3. Menumar: A natural born color change of two different colors in two areas, such as black and white colors or other colors which are not the normal color of the Esrog in two different areas of the Esrog.
4. Keminumar: A natural born color change of the same color in two areas.
5. A black Esrog.

- List of problematic natural born colors: Black; White; Dark Red; Dark Brown; Dark Blue
- List of valid natural born colors: Pink; Light Brown; Light Blue
- Apparent at first sight: A color change of any type is only able to invalidate an Esrog if it is noticeable to majority of people at first site. Meaning, that it is noticeable to the eye when it is held in one's hand [from a normal distance, at the first time] without needing to focus one's sight on it until he sees it.
- The law of color changes caused by thorns: The color change is only problematic if it occurred on its own with the growth of the Esrog. If, however, thorns punctured the Esrog and caused brown juice to come out and create red areas and indented areas within the Esrog, nevertheless it remains valid.
- Blet Lach-Leaf marks: A Blet Lach [leaf mark] is not considered a color change or blister and is thus valid even if it protrudes above the skin of the Esrog.
- What is the law if one's Esrog became brownish due to it being used by many people? The Esrog remains valid, and on the contrary, this is its beauty when it becomes browned due to the Mitzvah.
- Koshering an Esrog-Peeling off the color change: An Esrog that contains an invalidating color change may be validated/Koshered through peeling off the color from the Esrog. This is permitted to be done even initially. This applies even if the Esrog contains many areas of color changes. The following conditions, however, must be met for it to be considered Kosher through peeling off the color: One is to peel off only the external thin green skin of the Esrog in a way that the white body of the Esrog does not become revealed, thus assuring that nothing is missing from the body of the Esrog. [If the white skin of the Esrog becomes revealed, then it is invalid due to Chaser and possibly also due to Menumar.] After the invalidating color is peeled off, the color of the peeled area must be similar to the color of the rest of the Esrog for it to be Kosher.
- May one peel off a color change on Yom Tov? It is forbidden to peel a color change, or any other matter, off the Esrog on Yom Tov.
- If the green external peel of the Esrog has been removed, thus revealing the white underlying peel, but without removing any part of it, is the Esrog still valid?
- If the green external peel of the Esrog has been removed, thus revealing the white underlying peel, but without removing any part of it, is the Esrog still valid? Some Poskim rule that although the Esrog is not considered to be missing any piece, [and thus not invalid due to Chaser] it is viewed as containing a color change, and follows all of its invalidating rules. Other Poskim rule that the white rind of the Esrog is a natural color, and is not defined as a color change.

The Chotem

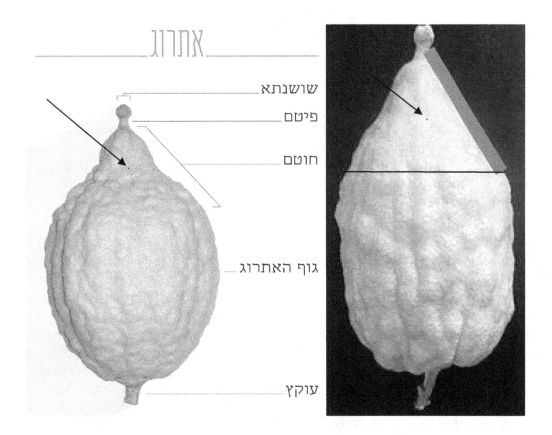

אתרוג

שושנתא
פיטם
חוטם

גוף האתרוג

עוקץ

G. Foul odor:
- An Esrog with a bad stench is invalid.

H. Cooked or soaked in water:
- A cooked Esrog is Pasul. Therefore, an Esrog which stayed submerged in water, or other liquids, for over 24 hours is considered cooked and is Pasul.

I. Shape:
- An Esrog which does not have the general Esrog shape, (i.e. round Esrog), is Pasul.

J. Size:
- An Esrog's minimum size is a Kibeitza, which is approximately 56 grams.

K. Unripe-Green/black:
- An Esrog which has not yet ripened to the point that part of it has begun to turn yellow is Pasul unless one is sure that the Esrog will reach this stage. The custom however is not to take such an Esrog even if certain that it will turn yellow, unless it has begun to turn yellow. [Ideally, however, the entire Esrog should look yellow. It is better to take a yellow Esrog with a Bletlach, than a green one which does not have Bletlach.]
- Black: A black colored Esrog is invalid. In those countries which generally grow green

Esrogim, this invalidation applies even if it has a slight black tint. However, in those countries that grow black Esrogim, a light black Esrog is valid being that this is the normal way of growth in these areas and it is not considered an abnormality. However, a very black Esrog which is similar in color to black colored people, is invalid even if it grows in Africa.

L. Pitam:

- Many Esrogim grow a wood stem protruding on their top called the Pitam or the dud. In many Esrogim, the Pitam begins to grow from within the inside of the Esrog. In others, it grows from its very top, on its outside. On the dud/Pitam grows a stem called the Shoshanta.

- Esrogim that grow without a Pitam: Many Esrogim grow without either a Pitam or Shoshanta and are nevertheless valid being that this is their normal way of growth, as they are formed this way from the beginning of their creation. One can identify an Esrog that grew without a Pitam through witnessing a groove or indentation on the top area where the Pitam usually grows.

- Pitam fell off: An Esrog which grew a Pitam and the Pitam fell off [such due to a blow and the like, as opposed to naturally while on the tree] then if any area of the Esrog's top is now revealed due to this area falling off, it is Pasul. This applies even if only part of the width of the Pitam fell off and revealed the area of the Esrog under that part while the other part remained on the Esrog. If, however, only the top part of the Pitam became removed while the bottom part of the Pitam has remained, and completely covers the area of the Esrog that the Pitam grew on, then the Esrog is valid. However, there are opinions who invalidate an Esrog with a missing Shoshanta as it is not Hadar. Practically, although we do not rule like this stringent opinion, nevertheless, it is proper to suspect for their words, and hence an Esrog with a missing Shoshanta should not be purchased if an Esrog of similar quality and beauty can be found. If, however, the Esrog with the missing Shoshanta is more beautiful than the other Esrogim, one should purchase this Esrog, as the main opinion follows the first opinion.

- On Chol Hamoed: During Chol Hamoed, an Esrog which was invalidated due to a fallen Pitam may be used [with a blessing] if absolutely no other Esrog is available.

- Second day in Diaspora: On the second day of Sukkos in the Diaspora, an Esrog which was invalidated due to a fallen Pitam, may be used if there is no other Esrog available. It is to be used without a Bracha.

M. Oketz/Stem:

- The Oketz is the stem from which the Esrog grows from on the tree.

- Fell off: If the Oketz was removed from the Esrog in a way that none of it remained on the Esrog, hence creating a grooved area, the Esrog is invalid. [Furthermore, even if only part of the Oketz fell off and revealed part of the groove, it is invalid.] However, if the stem has been cut in such a way that an entire sliver of it remains, and the groove of the Esrog is completely covered by this sliver, then the Esrog is valid. However, there are opinions who rule the Esrog is valid even if the entire Oketz was removed, as the Oketz is not part of the Esrog and hence cannot invalidate it due to a missing piece. Practically, although we do not rule like this lenient opinion, nevertheless, if no other Esrog is available one may rely on this opinion and use it. In such a case, one is allowed to use it with a blessing.

- On Chol Hamoed: On Chol Hamoed one may use an Esrog even if its stem has completely fallen off.

- Second day in Diaspora: On the second day of Sukkos in the Diaspora, an Esrog which was invalidated due to a fallen Oketz may be used if there is no other Esrog available. In such a case, it may be used with a Bracha.

N. Murkav/Grafted:

- A grafted Esrog, or a later generation of a grafted Esrog, is Pasul.
- The signs: There are four general signs in a kosher Esrog which are different in an Esrog grafted with lemon. 1) A grafted Esrog is smooth like a lemon while a kosher one is bumpy. 2) A grafted Esrog has its stem grown outside the Esrog's body while a kosher one has it indented into the Esrog. 3) A grafted Esrog has less peel and more juice while a kosher one has more peel and less juice. 4) A grafted Esrog has its seeds sitting horizontally while a kosher one has its seeds vertically.
- What is the status of a non-grafted Esrog which was born from the seed of a grafted Esrog? Some Poskim rule the Esrog is invalid. Other Poskim rule the Esrog is valid.
- Buying an Esrog that has tradition: Despite the above one should be careful to only buy an Esrog that has a tradition that it is not grafted. An example of such an Esrog is the Yanover which grows in southern Italy.

O. Calabria:

- There is a tradition handed from the Alter Rebbe to use specifically the Yanover Esrog for the Daled Minim for reasons known to him. It is called Yanover in reference to the region of growth in Italy. A possible reason for this tradition may be since Italy is referred to as the fat of the earth thus making its fruits have the most beauty.

P. Tithes-Using an Esrog from Eretz Yisrael:

- An Esrog which is forbidden to be eaten is not Kosher. Therefore, one must be certain that an Esrog from Israel has had all its tithes removed and is not Arlah (fruits grown within first three years of the tree).
- Esrogim from outside of Israel may be used even if they are from Arlah.

Q. Shemita Esrogim

- May one sell or purchase a Shemita Esrog? In the Sukkos of the eighth year the Esrog of Jewish owned fields in Eretz Yisrael is treated as Kedushas Shevi'is and hence may only be purchased through Otzer Beis Din, or Havlaah as explained next.
- Otzer Beis Din: A Halachically reliable Beis Din takes authority over the distribution of the fields Esrogim and collects a minimal fee for the Esrog in order to cover the expenses of the distribution.
- Havlaah: One may sell before Sukkos a Shemitah Esrog that is not Otzer Beis Din, if he does so in Havlaah. This means that one includes the sale of Shemitah produce within the sale of other products that are not from Shemitah. Thus, for example one may sell before Sukkos a Shemitah Esrog together with a bag of lemons. One may charge an over the market price for the bag of lemons, due to the included Esrog, if the Esrog is not given a specific price and is simply part of the package. The money received for this payment does not have Kedushas Shevi'is. [However, there are some Poskim that are stringent and prohibit selling even in Havlaah, and Havlaah in their opinion only helps in the fact that it does not give the money a status of Kedushas Shevi'is. Practically, the custom is to be lenient.]

- May one who is traveling to the Diaspora for Sukkos take with him an Israeli Esrog of Shemitah Otzer Beis Din? It is permitted to take one's personal Esrog with him to the Diaspora. One must make sure after Sukkos that the Esrog is properly guarded as Kedushas Shevi'is. Some Poskim write that one is to try to take the Esrog with him when he returns to Eretz Yisrael. Others rule this is not necessary.

- May one import Israeli Esrogim of Kedushas Shevi'is to the Diaspora for Sukkos? Some Poskim rule it is permitted to do so even initially, on condition that the Esrogim are sold Behavlaah. Other Poskim rule it is initially forbidden to do so. Some Poskim rule it is permitted to do so in a situation that the city will not have any Esrogim available if they are not sent. According to all, even if an Esrog was taken out of Eretz Yisrael in a forbidden manner, it remains Kosher and can be used for the Mitzvah.

- What is one to do with the Kedushas Shevi'is Esrog after Sukkos? One must guard the Esrog and may not discard it until it has spoiled and is no longer edible.

- Esrog Jam: It is permitted to make Esrog jam with an Esrog of Kedushas Shevi'is.

- Besamim: It is unclear if one may enter cloves into the Esrog and use it as Besamim.

- Must one perform Biur to Esrogim? Some Poskim rule one is not required to perform Biur to Esrogim of Kedushas Shevi'is. Other Poskim rule one is required to perform Biur to Esrogim. Even according to the stringent opinion, one is only required to perform Biur on Esrogim if he has the amount of Esrogim to suffice for three meals, which is over 1.5 Esrogim per family member.

- When is the Biur of Esrogim according to the stringent opinion? Some write the time of Biur for the Esrog is in Shevat. Others write the time of Biur is during Nissan.

Summary of conditions needed to be met for a Kosher Esrog:
1. No missing pieces.
2. No Chazazis or color change by Chotem.
3. No two Chazazis or two-color changes below Chotem.
4. Was not cooked.
5. Was not soaked in liquid for 24 hours.
6. Had its tithes removed.

---

5. The Hadassim

A. The identity of the Hadas:

- The Torah states that one is to take an Anaf Eitz Avos. This refers to a branch that grows leaves in a chain like braid form which covers most of the branch. This is unlike other branches in which the leaves do not braid or cover majority of the branch. This branch is referred to as the Hadas, myrtle.

- Is there a more preferable species of Hadassim? There are many species of Hadassim. Some have large leaves and others have short leaves. Some are particular to take only Tzefati Hadassim as they have many small leaves which fully cover the bark. Some Poskim rule that Hadassim with very wide and long leaves is a Hadas Shoteh.

- Must the leaves of the Hadas fully cover the bark and reach the leaves above it: This matter is disputed in Poskim. Some Poskim rule that if the leaves of the Hadas do not cover the bark, the Hadas is invalid. Thus, if a lower set of leaves do not reach the upper set of leaves, the Hadas is Pasul. Other Poskim completely negate this invalidation. Other Poskim rule that so long as majority of the bark is covered it is valid.

- The spiritual meaning of the Hadas: The Hadas is only valid if it contains a majority of three leave sets that grow on the same line. This is unlike other leaves of a branch, in which the leaves grow in a scattered method, along the branch. This pattern followed by the leaves of the Hadas is the aspect of unity found in this branch, over that of other branches. The Midrash explains that the Hadas represents the people who spend their time performing Mitzvos and Gemilus Chassadim, but do not learn Torah as a full occupation. Mitzvos correspond to the good smell found in the Hadas.

B. Length:

- The length of the Hadassim must be at least three Tefachim [24 cm.]

- How much is three Tefachim? Some Poskim rule that every Tefach is 4 Agudlin and hence three Tefachim is 12 Agudlin [24cm.]. Other Poskim rule that each Tefach is 3.33 Agudlin and hence three Tefach is 10 Agudlin [20 cm]. Practically, we are stringent to follow the first opinion of 24 cm. However, in a time of need, one may be lenient to use Hadassim of 20 cm. If one already used such a Hadas and then found one with 24 cm. He should shake it without a blessing being that he has already fulfilled his obligation according to one opinion.

- Is there a maximum length for the Hadas? No. The Hadassim may be as long as desired, although one must be careful that the Lulav spine always extends one Tefach above the Hadassim, and hence the longer the Hadas-the longer the Lulav must be.

C. Meshulash/Three Leaved:

- The Torah states that the Hadas must be braided. This means that there are three leaves that extend from each area of the branch, and that these three leaves are symmetric to each other, meaning that they extend from the same horizontal line. If two leaves are symmetric but the third leaf grows higher or lower than the other two, it is not considered braided. This form of Hadas is called a Hadas Shoteh and is invalid for use throughout all seven days of Sukkos. It may not be used even in a time of need that no other Hadas is available, even if one desires to take it without a blessing.

- How many leaves on the Hadas must be Meshulash? How many leaves on the Hadas must be Meshulash? Initially it is a Mitzvah to search for [i.e. purchase] a fully Meshulash Hadas.

This means that the Hadas should be Meshulash with three symmetric leaves by every set of leaves for its entire Shiur of three Tefachim. Nevertheless, even if the Hadas is not entirely Meshulash, if it is Meshulash for majority of its length then it may even initially be used with a blessing. This means that if majority of the sets of three leaves coming out of the branch have their stems coming out from the same horizontal line throughout the Shiur of three Tefachim, then the Hadas is valid and one may even initially recite a blessing over it. [This validation applies even if the head/top leaves of the Hadas is not Meshulash. If, however, majority of the Hadas is not Meshulash throughout its Shiur of three Tefach, the Hadas is invalid.]

- Must majority of the Shiur be Meshulash or majority of the entire branch? Example: If the Hadas is seven Tefachim long and is majority/fully Meshulash within its Shiur of three Tefachim, but is not Meshulash for the remaining four Tefachim, what is the law? Some Poskim rule we follow majority of the Shiur of three Tefachim and the Hadas is thus valid. Other Poskim, however, leave this matter in question. According to Admur, the Hadas is Kosher as rules the former opinion.

D. Leaves missing:
- If leaves fell off a Kosher Hadas, then as long as two leaves remain in majority of its sets within the Shiur of three Tefachim, it is Kosher. This applies even if the leaves of some of the sets have completely fallen off, [and even if the top leaves have fallen off], as long as there is still a majority of leaves in the majority of sets. If it does not contain two leaves in majority of its sets, it is invalid.
- If majority of the leaves droop downwards some Poskim rule the Hadas is invalid.
- If majority of the leaves are cut or broken to a few pieces, some Poskim rule the Hadas is invalid.

E. Top cut off:
- If the top of the Hadas [its branch and its leaves] were cut off, some Poskim rule the Hadas nevertheless remains valid. Other Poskim rule the Hadas is invalid. Practically, one should be stringent to use another Hadas, if it is available. If another Hadas is not available, then one may use it with a blessing. If the top leaves alone have been cut off [or fell off] but its stem is still intact, it may be used even initially. [Nevertheless, it is a Mitzvah Min Hamuvchar to use a Hadas which did not lose any of its top leaves.]

F. Dryness:
- If the leaves of a Hadas have dried, the Hadas is invalid. If, however it is not Halachically considered dry, even though the leaves have withered, it still remains valid.
- What is the definition of dry? If the leaves have dried to the point that they can be broken with one's nail and they have lost all their greenness, becoming white, it is Pasul. If the leaves have not lost their greenness, even if they look very dry and can be broken with a nail, they are still Kosher. [If they are dry and white but cannot be broken with a fingernail, they are still valid.]
- How many leaves must be dry to invalidate the Hadas? If the top leaves have remained completely fresh, then even if majority of the leaves have dried, they are still Kosher. However, if the top leaves have begun to whither and dry, even if they have not yet dried to the extent that invalidates them, some say it does not have the power to validate a Hadas

whose majority of leaves are dry and hence the Hadas is invalid. Other opinions rule that even a withered top leaf validates a dry Hadas. Practically, one should only rely on such a Hadas from the second day of Sukkos and onwards. If majority of the leaves [including the top] have dried to the point they can be broken with one's nail and have lost all their greenness, turning white, it is Pasul.

- <u>If only the top leaves are dry</u>: If the top leaves of the Hadas have dried to the extent to make them Pasul, some opinions rule the Hadas nevertheless remains valid. Others rule it is invalid, even if the rest of the leaves have remained fresh. Practically one should be stringent to use another Hadas if it is available. If another Hadas is not available, then one may use it with a blessing.

- <u>On Chol Hamoed</u>: Even if the top leaves have begun to dry, as long as they are not completely dry, the Hadas is Kosher even if majority of its other leaves have dried.

- <u>Second day of Diaspora</u>: On the second day of Sukkos in the Diaspora if no other Hadas is available one may use a Hadas whose leaves have dried so long as its top is not completely dry. One is to use it without a Bracha.

G. Random leaves which grow wild on the Hadas:

- Some Poskim rule that random leaves or branches which grow on the Hadas and interfere with its sets of Meshulash leaves, can possibly invalidate the Hadas and are to be plucked off. Other Poskim rule that there is no need to be particular to remove the random leaves, and that so is the custom. Practically, it is proper initially to be stringent to remove these leaves from before Yom Tov. The above dispute only applies to leaves that grow amongst the actual sets of the three Meshulash leaves. However, leaves/branches that sporadically grow between sets, according to all do not need to be removed.

6. The Aravos

A. The identity of the Aravah:

- The Torah states that one is to take an Arvei Nachal. This refers to the willow branch. Although majority of Aravos grow near banks of water they are valid from all areas, even if they grow in a desert or mountain, being that they have all the signs.

- Its spiritual meaning: The Aravah is a big bushy tree that has its branches and leaves grow very close to each other. This represents brotherhood, and it was thus chosen for the Mitzvah of unity. The Midrash explains that the Aravah represents the people who do not contain either Mitzvos or good deeds, as the Aravah contains neither a good taste, nor smell. On the Holiday of Sukkos, all Jews unify together, including such Jews. The Baal Shem tov explains that the Aravah represents the simple Jew, who serves Hashem with utter simplicity.

B. Its Signs:

- The following are the signs of a Kosher Aravah: 1) A red stem: This means that the Aravah comes from a tree that grows red stems. Thus, even if the branch is currently still green due to lack of sunlight, nevertheless it is valid, as it will eventually become red due to the sun. 2) The leaves are shaped like a brook; narrow and long. 3) Leaves that have smooth edges, not serrated like a saw. If the leaves have tiny serrations, they are still considered smooth edged. If, however, the serrations are large they are invalid. The Aravah must have all three signs to be Kosher. An Aravah that has red stems and long narrow leaves, but has large serrations, is invalid.

- Aravah branch with leaves growing on small branches as opposed to stem: An Aravah stem which contains small branches on which the leaves grow, does not need to have these leaves and branches removed. Furthermore, the Aravah remains Kosher even if it has no leaves growing on the actual stem but rather only on its branches. Nonetheless, it is proper for it to also contain some leaves on the branch.

C. Its length:

- The length of the Aravos must be at least three Tefachim. Some Poskim rule that every Tefach is 4 Agudlin and hence three Tefachim is 12 Agudlin [24 cm.] Other Poskim rule that each Tefach is 3.33 Agudlin and hence three Tefach is 10 Agudlin [20 cm]. Practically, we are stringent to follow the first opinion of 24 cm. However, in a time of need, one may be lenient to use an Aravah of 20 cm. If one already used such an Aravah and then found one with 24 centimeters, he should shake it without a blessing being that he has already fulfilled his obligation.

- Is there a maximum length for the Aravah? No. The Aravos may be as long as desired, although one must be careful that the Lulav spine always extends one Tefach above the Aravos. [Thus, the longer the Aravah, the longer the Lulav must be. If the Aravah is too long and hence covers the top one Tefach area of the spine of the Lulav, then the Aravah is to be shortened from its bottom.]

D. Top Cut:

- If the top of the Aravah was cut off, it is Pasul. This refers to that the actual wood branch of the Aravah became cut and not just its top leaf. Therefore, if the Aravos are very long, one must beware to cut it specifically on the bottom of the Aravah and not the top.

- The Lavluv: If the upper Lavluv leaf was cut off, the Aravah nevertheless remains Kosher as the Lavluv is a mere leaf and only when the actual branch is cut is the Aravah invalidated. Nevertheless, some are accustomed to buy Aravos with a Lavluv, as the Lavluv proves that the top of the Aravah is still intact and has not been cut.
- If the top of the Aravah is folded over is it Kosher? Yes.

E. Leaves fell off:
- Bedieved-Letter of law: If majority of the Aravah leaves fell off. the Aravah is Pasul. One must be very careful regarding this matter, as it occurs that upon inserting the Aravos into the [binding of the] Lulav, and likewise upon shaking the Lulav, that leaves fall off. [It is thus advisable to check the Aravos daily to verify they still contain majority leaves. Likewise, it is advised to purchase a number of sets of Aravos on Erev Sukkos, which can be used in a case of need throughout Sukkos. When replacing the Aravos, one is not to stick the new Aravos into the knot of the Lulav, and rather one is to undo the knots and then place the new Aravos inside.]
- If only minority of the leaves fell off, the Aravah is valid.
- Lechatchila-Mitzvah Min Hamuvchar: It is a Mitzvah Min Hamuvchar to take an Aravah which contains all its leaves. Thus, although a majority leaved Aravah is valid, as explained above, nevertheless, Lechatchila one is not to take such an Aravah if finding a fully leaved Aravah of which none of its leaves fell off, is easily attainable.
- Must majority of the Shiur [i.e. 24 cm] still contain leaves or majority of the entire branch? Example: If the Aravah is seven Tefachim long and is majority/fully leaved within its Shiur of three Tefachim, but is not leaved for the remaining four Tefachim, what is the law? We follow majority of the Shiur of 24 centimeters and not majority of the branch.
- If the Aravah was originally Kosher, and the leaves fell off as a result of the shaking, is the Aravah now invalid? The Aravah is invalid if majority of its leaves fell off as a result of the shaking. However, some Poskim suggest that the invalidation of an Aravah due to the falling of its leaves is only in the event that one did not yet fulfill the Mitzvah with it. If, however, one already fulfilled the Mitzvah of Daled Minim with this Aravah, such as on the 1st day of Sukkos, then it remains Kosher throughout Chol Hamoed even if the leaves fall off due to the shaking. Based on this suggestion, we can justify the custom of many to not bother to inspect the validity of the Aravos and its state of intact leaves throughout Chol Hamoed. Practically, one is to not rely on this approach, and is to perform a daily inspection of his Aravah prior to doing the Mitzvah to verify its Kashrus state.
- Directives for Mivtzaim: Those fulfilling the great and holy Mitzvah, and directive of the Rebbe, to merit other Jews with the shaking of Daled Minim, must be very careful to periodically verify throughout the day that their Aravos remain intact with majority of leaves. This especially applies when people shake the Lulav in a very strong way. A number of sets of Aravos should be brought with the person so he can change the branches as deemed necessary.
- If the leaves droop downwards: If majority of the leaves have become detached from their original place of growth and hence droop down, they are invalid, even though they still remain slightly attached to the actual stem.
- Leaves have split: If majority of the leaves have split in two, in majority of their length, the Aravah is Pasul.

F. Dry Leaves:
- If majority of the leaves have dried it is invalid.
- <u>Definition</u>: The definition of dry is if the leaves have dried to the extent they lost their coloring and have turned white. If they have not yet turned white, they are valid even if they are dried to the point they are withered [and can be broken with one's finger nail].

Chapter 3: The Laws and customs of the Holiday

1. Erev Sukkos

A. Increasing in charity:
- One should increase in Tzedakah on Erev Sukkos. This includes inviting over the poor for meals.

B. Purchasing Jewelry and clothing:
- It is a Biblical positive command and obligation for one to rejoice and be of happy spirit on Yom Tov. This obligation applies to oneself, his wife, his children and his entire household [even non-relatives]. The head of the household is responsible for rejoicing his household during this time. One is to buy his wife [and adult female children and other adult female household members] jewelry or clothing in accordance to his affordability. If one cannot afford to purchase clothing or jewelry, then he is to purchase them new shoes in order to fulfill this Mitzvah.]

C. Baking Challahs:
- One is to bake Challahs for Yom Tov which will be used for Lechem Mishneh and is not to buy them at the bakery as is done during the week, just as is the law on Erev Shabbos. This matter of baking one's own Challah is included in the honoring of Yom Tov. One is not to divert from this custom.
- How much is one to bake? One is to bake at least the amount that requires one to remove Challah from the dough.

D. Bodily preparations:
- Cutting the nails: It is a Mitzvah to cut one's nails on Erev Sukkos in honor of Yom Tov, just as is the law on Erev Shabbos. [One is to cut his nails prior to immersing.]
- Getting a haircut on Erev Sukkos: It is a Mitzvah upon each person [who did not get a haircut on Erev Rosh Hashanah] to get a haircut on Erev Sukkos in honor of Yom Tov, in order so one does not enter into the holiday looking unrepresentable. It is permitted to get a haircut throughout the entire day of Erev Sukkos, even past the time of Mincha. This applies even to a professional haircut that is being done by a Jew in exchange for payment.
- Bathing on Erev Sukkos: It is a Mitzvah to bathe one's body in hot water on Erev Sukkos in honor of Yom Tov.

E. Eating past the 10th hour of the day:
- It is forbidden to eat [a meal] from Mincha and onwards [i.e. the 10th hour of the day] until the start of Yom Tov. [This is approximately three hours before sunset]. The above is only with regards to a set meal [i.e. 55 grams of bread], however, it is permitted to eat a mere snack up until sunset and there is no need to refrain from doing so. If one transgressed or forgot and did not eat prior to the 10th hour, then on Erev Sukkos he may not eat a meal past the 10th hour.

F. Inviting the needy to one's meal:

- It is an obligation for one to invite orphans, widows and those which are in need to the Yom Tov meals. If one does not do so then it is not considered a meal eaten in honor of the Mitzvah but rather for the satiation of his abdomen.

G. Eiruv Tavshilin:

- Whenever Sukkos falls on Thursday [in the Diaspora], one performs an Eiruv Tavshilin on Erev Sukkos [Wednesday] in the Diaspora. The owner of the house takes a whole loaf/role of bread/Matzah the size of a Kibeitza [which is to later be used on Shabbos] and a Kezayis of a cooked piece of meat or other food which one eats together with bread. If one has another person to use to acquire the food to him on behalf of the city then the owner is to say:

אני מזכה לכל'מי שרוצה לזכות ולסמוך על ערוב זה

- The person who is acquiring the food for the townspeople then lifts the food up one Tefach. The owner then takes back the food and recites the following blessing: [If one does not have another person to use to acquire the food to the townspeople then he is to simply hold the food and begin from here with the following blessing:]

ברוך אתה ה' אלוקינו מלך העולם אשר קדשנו במצותיו וצונו על מצות עירוב.

- After the blessing one says in a language that he understands "With this Eiruv it will be permitted for us to bake and cook and insulate foods, and light candles and to do all our needs on Yom Tov for Shabbos".

בדין יהא שרא לנא לאפויי ולבשולי ולאטמוני ולאדלוקי שרגא ולתקנא ולמעבד כל צרכנא מיומא טבא לשבתא לנא ולכל ישראל הדרים בעיר הזאת

H. Binding the Lulav:

- One should bind the Lulav in the Sukkah. One should be meticulous to bind the Lulav himself as opposed to having someone else do it for him.

I. Verifying the validity of the Sukkah:

- Before leaving to Shul for Mincha on Erev Sukkos one is to verify the validity of the Sukkah and confirm that everything is in order. If one's Sukkah contains an awning to protect from rain, it is to be opened before Yom Tov.

J. Candle lighting:

- One first lights the candles and then says the blessing of "Baruch Ata Hashem Elokeinu Melech Haolam Asher Kidishanu Bimitzvosav Vetzivanu Lehadlik Neir Shel Yom Tov". This blessing is then followed by the blessing of Shehechiyanu.
- When are the candles lit? The custom is to light the candles prior to sunset at the same time that they are lit on Erev Shabbos. [One who did not light the candles prior to sunset is to light the candles at night, on Yom Tov, from a preexisting flame. It is to be lit at the very least prior to the return of the men from Shul.]
- Where are the candles to be lit: The candles are to be lit within the Sukkah. If this is not

possible [such as due to safety reasons] then one is to light inside.

- <u>If a man is lighting candles when is he to say the blessing of Shehechiyanu, by lighting or by Kiddush?</u> A man always says the blessing of Shehechiyanu by Kiddush and not by candle lighting, even in the event that he is lighting candles. However, in such a case he is to light candles directly before Kiddush, hence having the blessing of Shehechiyanu also go on the candle lighting. If, however he said the blessing by candle lighting he does not repeat the blessing by Kiddush. [However, on the first night of Sukkos this only applies if he lit the candles in the Sukkah. Otherwise he must repeat Shehechiyanu for the sake of the Mitzvah of Sukkah that he is now fulfilling by Kiddush.]
- <u>Preparing a 24-hour candle:</u> It is proper to prepare a 24-hour candle on Erev Sukkos in order to have a preexisting flame available to use on Yom Tov.

2. The First day[s] of Yom Tov:

A. The Yom Tov night meal:
- <u>The Seder of Kiddush on the first night:</u> Men are to make Kiddush inside the Sukkah even if it is raining. The order of Kiddush on the first night of Sukkos is Askinu, Hagafen, Asher Bachar Banu, Leisheiv, and then Shehechiyanu. The Rebbe's custom is to look at Sechach upon saying the blessing of Leisheiv.
- <u>Having the Sukkah in mind by Shehechiyanu of first night:</u> The blessing of Shehechiyanu said during Kiddush on the first night of Sukkos includes both the holiday and the Mitzvah of dwelling in the Sukkah. [Thus, upon saying Shehechiyanu during Kiddush one is to intend to include also the Holiday and also the Sukkah.] It is for this reason that on the first night, the blessing of Shehechiyanu is said before the blessing of Leisheiv, as it also includes the Mitzvah of Sukkah.
- <u>The Seder of Kiddush on the second night in Diaspora:</u> The order of Kiddush on the second night of Sukkos is Askinu, Hagafen, Asher Bachar Banu, Shehechiyanu and then Leisheiv.
- <u>Dip Challah in honey:</u> It is customary of some to dip it in honey throughout all the Yom Tov [and Shabbos] meals until Simchas Torah.
- <u>Leisheiv Basukkah for the household:</u> It is customary for the household members which heard Kiddush to say the blessing of Leisheiv Basukkah after saying the blessing of Hamotzi.
- <u>How much to eat:</u> A man must eat over a Kibeitza of bread in the Sukkah on 1st [and 2nd night in the Diaspora].
- <u>When to eat:</u> One is to beware to eat the meal before midnight.
- <u>What is the law if in Kiddush one accidently recited Mikadeish Hashabbos instead of Mikadeish Yisrael Vehazmanim?</u> If one remembered prior to the amount of time of saying the words "Shalom Aleichem Rebbe" from passing, and he has not yet begun saying the next blessing, he is to correct himself and say "Mikadeish Yisrael Vehazmanim". If the above amount of time has already passed, or one already said the first word of the next blessing, he is to repeat from the start of the blessing of Asher Bachar Banu. If, however, he has already said the blessing of Shehechiyanu or Leisheiv Basukkah he is not to repeat this blessing of Shehechiyanu or Leisheiv.

B. Detailed laws of the blessing of Shehechiyanu:

- The blessing of Shehechiyanu is recited after the completion of Kiddush, prior to drinking the wine, as explained above. In the Diaspora, it is recited in Kiddush of both the first and second night of Sukkos. [One who recited the blessing of Shehechiyanu during candle lighting may not repeat the blessing during Kiddush. Thus, women who are saying Kiddush do not say the blessing of Shehechiyanu if they recited it by candle lighting. If a man is lighting the candles, then he should say the Shehechiyanu by Kiddush. If he said it by candle lighting then he does not repeat the blessing by Kiddush, as explained next.]

- What is the law if a man said Shehechiyanu upon lighting candles? If one said the blessing by candle lighting, he does not repeat the blessing by Kiddush. However, on the first night of Sukkos, this only applies if he lit the candles in the Sukkah. Otherwise he must repeat Shehechiyanu for the sake of the Mitzvah of Sukkah that he is now fulfilling by Kiddush.

- Forgot Shehechiyanu: One who forgot to recite the blessing of Shehechiyanu [during Kiddush, prior to drinking the wine, is to recite it afterwards, immediately upon remembering.] Even if he only remembered the next day, he is to recite Shehechiyanu. It may be recited even without a cup of wine. [Ideally, it may be recited anywhere upon remembering, even if he is in middle of the marketplace.] however on Sukkos, when he says Shehechiyanu, he needs to say it inside the Sukkah, in order to exempt also the Sukkah with the blessing. [If in the Diaspora one did not remember to recite Shehechiyanu until the second night of Yom Tov began, then he fulfills his blessing of Shehechiyanu of the first night through the Shehechiyanu recited after Kiddush of the second night.] If he forgot to say the blessing of Shehechiyanu on the first day, and [in the Diaspora] also forgot to say it during Kiddush of the second night, then he is obligated to recite the blessing whenever he remembers throughout the seven days of Sukkos. [This applies until the end of Hoshana Raba. Once Shemini Atzeres begins, Shehechiyanu can no longer be recited.]

- Said Shehechiyanu outside of the Sukkah: In any case that the blessing of Shehechiyanu was said outside the Sukkah, such as if one said Kiddush in his house, then the blessing of Shehechiyanu must be repeated upon the next time he eats a meal in the Sukkah. It is said after the blessing of Leisheiv is recited.

C. Guests:

- The Mitzvah: It is a Mitzvah and obligation to host paupers, orphans, widows and other unfortunate individual's as guests for one's Yom Tov meals. One who refuses to do so, is not considered to be having a meal of a Mitzvah, but rather a one of abomination.

- Gentile guests: It is forbidden to invite gentile guests on Yom Tov, for the Yom Tov meal. If, however, the gentile arrived on his own, one may offer him and give him to eat, although it is forbidden to press on the gentile to eat if he does not accept the initial offer.

- Housemaid: It is permitted to have a gentile housemaid eat the Yom Tov meals with one's family.

- May one allow a gentile to enter one's Sukkah? One should not invite a gentile into the Sukkah as this causes the holiness to leave. Therefore, one should not have a gentile maid clean the Sukkah inside.

D. Ushpizin:

- The Zohar states that during Sukkos we merit to have the seven shepherds of Israel as guests in our Sukkah, upon dwelling within it. One is required to rejoice each day with the Ushpizin of that day.

- <u>The order:</u> The seven Ushpizin are: Avraham, Yitzchak, Yaakov, Moshe, Aaron, Yosef, David. Some, however, place Yosef before Moshe. All seven guests come each of the seven days of Sukkos to visit each Jew in his Sukkah, however, each day there is a different leader who sits at the head.

- <u>The Yehi Ratzon prayer:</u> Some write that one must verbally invite the Ushpizin in order to bring them into one's Sukkah. Some are accustomed to reciting a special prayer of Yehi Ratzon for the Ushpizin of that day. Practically, it is not the Chabad custom to say the Yehi Ratzon for the Ushpizin, however one should mention a Dvar Torah involving the guest of that night.

- <u>The Chassidic Ushpizin:</u> There is a tradition amongst the Chabad Rabbeim that in addition to the classical seven Ushpizin of Avraham, Yitzchak, and Yaakov etc., on each night the Chassidic Rabbeim also come to visit, starting with the Baal Shem Tov until the Rebbe Rashab.

E. Birchas Hamazon:

- <u>Ya'aleh Veyavo:</u> One recites Ya'aleh Veyavo within Birchas Hamazon on Yom Tov.

- <u>Forgot to recite:</u> If one forgot to say Ya'aleh Veyavo in the Birchas Hamazon of the Yom Tov night meal or the first Yom Tov day meal, and only remembered after he already began the first word "Baruch" of the blessing of Hatov Vehameitiv [and certainly if he already finished Birchas Hamazon], then he is required to repeat from the beginning of Birchas Hamazon. [This applies for both men and women. If one is in doubt if he said it, we assume he did not say it and he must repeat Birchas Hamazon.]

- <u>Remembered after the blessing of Uvinei Yerushalyim, but prior to beginning Hatov Vehameitiv:</u> All the above refers to a case that one already began the first word "Baruch" of the next blessing. If, however, one remembered to recite Yaleh Veyavo after completing "Uvinei Yerushalyim" but prior to beginning the first word of the next blessing, then in all cases [i.e. whether night or day meal, and whether the first, second or third meal] he is to say the following blessing:

ברוך אתת ה' אלקינו מלך העולם אשר נתן ימים טובים לעמו ישראל לששון ולשמחה את יום חג הסוכות הזה. ברוך אתה ה' מקדש ישראל והזמנים:

- If he does not know how the blessing begins and concludes then in such a case, he must repeat from the beginning of Birchas Hamazon [by the night and first day meal].

- <u>Yom Tov that coincides with Shabbos:</u> In the event that Sukkos falls on Shabbos, one is to say both Ritzei and Ya'aleh Veyavo. If one forgot to say both Ritzei and Ya'aleh Veyavo and remembered prior to beginning the word Baruch, then he is to say:

ברוך אתת ה' אלקינו מלך העולם שנתן שבתות למנוחה לעמו לישראל באהבה לאות ולברית וימים לששון ולשמחה את יום חג הסוכות הזה. ברוך אתת ה' מקדש השבת וישראל והזמנים.

- If one forgot to say only Ritzei or only Ya'aleh Veyavo then he only mentions the additional blessing of the skipped part. If one already said the word "Baruch" or already finished Birchas Hamazon, then he must repeat from the beginning and say both Ritzei and Ya'aleh Veyavo even though he already said one of them the first time. [If he forgot to say Ritzei this second time it is questionable whether he fulfills his obligation and it is thus best to wash again on a Kezayis of bread and recite Birchas Hamazon.]

- <u>What is he to do if he remembers to say Yaleh Veyavo in the midst of the Bracha of "Boneh Berachamav Yerushalayim"?</u> If he remembered prior to saying the words "Boneh

Berachamav Yerushalyim" some Poskim rule he should end the blessing with Lamdeini Chukecha and then repeat from Yaleh Veyavo.

- Harachaman: By the Harachamans one recites the Harachaman for Yom Tov "Harachaman Hu Yanchileinu Leyom Shekulo Tov". Afterwards one recites the Harachaman for Sukkos "Harachaman Hu Yakim Lanu Es Sukkas Dovid Hanofeles". On Shabbos Sukkos one recites first the Harachaman for Shabbos and then the Harachaman for Yom Tov and then the Harachaman for Sukkos.
- Meiyn Shalosh-Al Hamichya: One adds the following words when reciting the after blessing of Meiyn Shalosh on Yom Tov: "Vezachreinu Letovah Beyom Chag Hasukkos Hazeh"
- What is the law if one forgot to say "Vezachreinu Letovah" in Meiyn Shalosh [Al Hamichya; Al Hapeiros; Al Hagafen]? One does not have to repeat the after blessing. This applies even when reciting an Al Hagafen after Kiddush. If one remembered prior to reciting the concluding blessing of "Baruch Ata Hashem" some Poskim rule one is to retract and recite the addition.

F. Simchas Beis Hashoeiva:
- Simchas Beis Hashoeiva begins on the 1st night of Sukkos. See Halacha 3F!

G. Shaking Lulav:
- When: One is to awake early to fulfill the Mitzvah of Daled Minim especially on the first day of Sukkos. From the letter of the law, one is to fulfill the Mitzvah of shaking Lulav before Hallel. However, since it is a Mitzvah Min Hamuvchar to shake the Lulav in the Sukkah, and one cannot leave the Shul in the interim, therefore in the morning prior to prayer one is to say the blessing over the Lulav in the Sukkah
- Where: One is to shake the Lulav inside the Sukkah, as stated above.
- Eating: It is forbidden to eat before shaking the Lulav. If, however, one will not be able to shake until after midday he should eat beforehand. It is customary even for women not to eat at all until they shake Lulav. From the letter of the law, however, women are allowed to eat up to 55 grams of Mezonos, unlimited amount of fruit and vegetables, and unlimited number of beverages. This certainly applies to a woman who is pregnant, nursing or feels weak. However, she should not eat a full meal or over 55 grams of Mezonos until she shakes Lulav. If, however, they feel that they require this amount of food to eat then it is completely allowed.
- How: See Chapter 2 Halacha 1F!

H. Hallel-General Laws:
- The complete Hallel is recited throughout all 8/9 days of Sukkos and Shemini Atzeres with a blessing. This applies whether one is with a Minyan or Davening in private. If a Minyan is present, there is no Halachic precedence, and one can to choose to say the blessing himself, or be Yotzei with the Chazan, as each option contains an advantageous aspect. Nonetheless, the widespread custom today is for every individual to recite the blessing himself, even if a Minyan is present, and so is the proper directive. Some recite it prior to the Chazan and hence complete it prior to the Chazan completing his blessing. Others recite it together with the Chazan and some recite it after the Chazan. Those who recite it after the Chazan, must intend to not be Yotzei the blessing with his recital.

- Women: Women are exempt from reciting Hallel. Nevertheless, they are permitted to recite it even with a blessing.
- When: Hallel may be recited throughout the entire day, from dawn [Alos Hashachar] until nightfall [Tzeis Hakochavim]. Thus, if one did not recite Hallel immediately after Davening [Shemoneh Esrei of] Shacharis, he may recite it throughout the day, until Tzeis Hakochavim.
- Reading Hallel with the congregation prior to Shacharis? One is to be particular to read Hallel together with the congregation immediately after Shemoneh Esrei. If one is holding prior to Davening, some Poskim rule he is to stop and recite Hallel together with the congregation. This applies for Hallel of all days. Nevertheless, the Arizal was not comfortable with such an arrangement of reciting Hallel out of its proper order, and hence according to the Arizal one is never to read Hallel prior to Davening. [No clear directive has been given with regards to the Chabad custom in whether one should say Hallel with the congregation prior to his Davening, if the circumstance occurs. Nevertheless, it is known that the Chabad Rebbeim would be careful to always pray with the same pace as the Minyan on Yom Tov in order to say Hallel with the congregation. This is despite the Rebbeim's usual practice of praying at greater length than the Minyan. Practically, the widespread custom amongst Chabad Chassidim is not to recite it before Davening.] If one is holding within Pesukei Dezimra, he is not to stop and recite Hallel together with the congregation on days that the complete Hallel is recited.
- Hefsek-Making an interval to answer Amen and the like: When the complete Hallel is recited, the laws of making a Hefsek [speech interval] during Hallel has the same laws as a Hefsek during the reading of the morning Shema. This applies for both the laws of Hefsek within individual paragraphs and between paragraphs.
- Standing for Hallel: Hallel is to be recited in a standing position. It is forbidden for one to lean on any item during Hallel [in a way that it supports him from falling]. If one transgressed and recited Hallel in a sitting position, he nevertheless fulfills his obligation and is not required to repeat the recital of Hallel.

I. The Lulav during Hallel:

- From the letter of the law, one is to fulfill the Mitzvah of shaking Lulav before Hallel. However, since it is a Mitzvah Min Hamuvchar to shake the Lulav in the Sukkah, and one cannot leave the Shul in the interim, therefore in the morning prior to prayer one is to say the blessing over the Lulav while still in the Sukkah.
- Holding the Lulav and Esrog: The Lulav is held throughout the entire duration of Hallel. The current Chabad custom is to only lift the Esrog at the times that it needs to be shaken. In Hakhel years, the custom is to hold both the Lulav and Esrog together throughout the duration of Hallel.
- Shaking Lulav: We shake the Lulav a total of four times in Hallel, each time shaking it 18 times [three times in each of the six direction, for a total of 72 shakes]. One shakes the Lulav one time by the first Hodu Lahashem, and one time by Ana Hashem Hoshia Na'ah, and a second time by the repeated Ana Hashem Hoshia Na'ah, and one time by the first Hodu Lahashem of the second set. One who said a blessing on the Lulav after Shacharis, prior to Hallel, is to only shake the Lulav three times in Hallel, omitting the shaking in the 2nd Ana Hashem.
- If one did not have a Lulav until the midst of Hallel, he is to recite a blessing over the Lulav during Hallel.

Hodu LaHashem

Word	Direction
Hodu	South [right]
LaHashem	nothing
Ki	North [left]
Tov	East [front]
Ki	Up
Leolam	Down
Chasdo	West [back]

Ana Hashem

Word	Direction
Ana	South [right] North [Left]
Hashem	nothing
Hoshia	East [front] Up
Naah	Down West [back]

J. Hoshanos:

- Throughout all the days of Sukkos, immediately after Hallel, prior to Kaddish Shaleim, it is customary to say Hoshanos [with exception to Shabbos, as explained below]. Each day during Hoshanos one is to circle the Bimah one time while holding on to the Lulav [and Esrog] and one recites a single Hoshana. On Hoshana Raba one circles the Bimah seven times and says seven Hoshanos. The circling is done in memory of the encircling of the Mizbeiach that took place in the times of the Mikdash.

- <u>The direction:</u> The Hakafos are performed towards the right side [i.e. counterclockwise]. [One is to do a full circle, and not cut through the Bima to shorten the length.]

- <u>How to hold the Lulav and Esrog:</u> One is to hold the Lulav and Esrog in two separate hands, the Lulav in his right hand and the Esrog in his left. [The Lulav and Esrog is held close to the heart. It is to be held until the completion of the Hoshanos.]

- <u>One who does not have a Lulav:</u> One without a Lulav does not encircle the Bima for Hoshanos. [This applies even by Hoshanah Raba.]

- <u>The Sifrei Torah:</u> It is customary to place a Sefer Torah on the Bima while encircling it. [Some Poskim rule that the Sefer Torah is to be held rather than rest on the Bima. The custom is that if there is someone present who does not have a Lulav and will thus not be encircling the Bima, then he is to be given the Sefer Torah to hold. The Aron remains open throughout the Hoshanos.]

- <u>How it is done:</u> The Chabad custom is to say the word Hoshana prior to each one of the words said for that day. The words are said silently by both the congregation and Chazan, without encircling the Bima, until the words that begin with a Samech or Ayin. Upon reaching the words that begin with a Samech or Ayin, one says Hoshana prior and post each word, repeating after the Chazan, and only then begins to encircle the Bima. [The worldly custom, however, is for the Chazan to begin reciting aloud from the first Hoshana, and to begin the encircling from the first letter Alef.]

- <u>Avel/Mourner:</u> A mourner does not encircle the Bimah by Hoshanos. This applies both to an Onen, or one who is within the 12-month period after the passing of his father or mother. [It likewise applies to a mourner within thirty days of the passing of one of the other seven other relatives. However, some Poskim are lenient to allow a mourner for other relatives to perform the Hakafah.]

- Shabbos: One does not encircle the Bima on Shabbos, and one does not place the Sefer Torah on the Bima. Some Poskim rule that the paragraph of Hoshanos is likewise omitted on Shabbos, however, the widespread custom is to say it [without encircling or removing a Sefer Torah]. [Practically, the Chabad custom is not to recite the Hoshanos on Shabbos. On Sunday, one recites the Hoshanos of that day, and the skipped Hoshanos of Shabbos, although we only encircle the Bima once.]
- One who is Davening without a Minyan: It is accustomed to performing Hoshanos in Shul around the Bima even if one is Davening without a Minyan. Likewise, one who is Davening at home may place a Tanach on a table or chair and perform the Hakafos.

K. The reading of the Torah:
- Moshe Rabbeinu established for the Jewish people that on every Yom Tov one is to read the Torah portion dealing with that Holiday. The Sages of the Mishneh and Gemara chose the exact portion of the Torah that is read on each holiday.
- The amount of Aliyos: Moshe instituted that five men be called up for an Aliyah by the Torah reading of Yom Tov.
- Haftorah: The reading of the Haftorah was instituted by the Anshei Kneses Hagedola. They instituted that one should read from Navi on every holiday from a portion that deals with the holiday events. The Sages of the Mishneh and Gemara chose the exact portion of Navi that is read on each holiday.
- The Maftir: [Maftir in truth refers to the reading of the portion from Navi formally known as the Haftorah. It comes from the word Petor which means finish, as the reading is completed with the Haftorah.] However, the person that reads the Maftir from Navi is also required to first read a section from the Torah. In the times of the Sages of the Mishneh and Talmud the Maftir would read from the Torah as part of the five Aliyos that were read from the portion of that Holiday which was read from the first Torah scroll. [There was hence no second scroll taken out from the ark] However, in later generations, the Rabanan Savuraiy established, and so was accustomed by the Geonim which followed them, that the Maftir is to read [from a second scroll] the portion of the Musaf sacrifice written in Parshas Pinchas. This institution was based on the following teaching of the Sages: Avraham stated in front of Hashem "Master of the world when the Temple is not in existence the children of Israel do not have on what to find support. What will be with my children when they sin? Perhaps you will do to them as you did to the generation of the Mabul and Haflaga. Hashem answered "I have already established for them the order of the Karbanos. When the Karbanos are read, I consider it as if they sacrificed the Karban before me and I forgive all of their sins.
- Two Torah scrolls: Being that two different sections of the Torah need to be read on Yom Tov; therefore, one is initially required to remove two Torah scrolls; one for the Holiday reading, and the second for the Maftir. It does not suffice to remove only one Torah scroll and then roll it to the Parsha of Musafim [for Maftir]. [The scrolls are to be rolled to their proper places prior to Davening. Doing so is not to be delayed until Kerias Hatorah. If only one scroll is available, then the two portions are to be read from the same scroll.]
- Yud Gimmel Middos-Hashem Hashem: When the Shalosh Regalim fall on a weekday the 13 attributes [i.e. passage of Hashem Hashem] is recited one time when the Ark is opened to remove the Torah scrolls, prior to Berich Shmei. If Yom Tov falls on Shabbos, the Yud

Gimmel Middos [and Ribono Shel Olam] is not recited. After the recital of Hashem one recites the prayer of Ribono Shel Olam [one time]. [Likewise, the verse of Veani Sefilasi, which is recited after the Ribono Shel Olam is only recited one time.] This is then followed by the prayer of Berich Shmei.

- <u>The reading on first day of Sukkos</u>: On the first day of Sukkos, after reciting Hallel, two Torah scrolls are removed from the Aron. The Torah scroll is to be rolled to its proper section before Davening in order to prevent delay for the congregation. By the first scroll, five men are called up for Aliyos and the portion from the Parsha of Emor "Shur Oi Kesev" is read. [After the above reading, the second scroll is placed on the Bima which is followed by half Kaddish. Hagba is then done to the first scroll. The Mi Shebeirach for the ill is recited after Hagba. One may not open the second scroll until the first scroll is rolled up and placed in its Meil. When the scrolls are being returned to the Aron, the scroll of Maftir is taken first.]

- <u>The reading on second day of Sukkos</u>: The reading on the second day in the Diaspora follows the same order as on the first day, with the same reading as the first day repeated from the first scroll and the same reading of Maftir repeated in the second scroll.

- <u>The Maftir</u>: For Maftir of Sukkos one reads from the second Torah scroll the portion of "Ubachamisha Asar Yom" found in the Parsha of Pinchas. After Maftir, one performs Hagba to the second scroll and reads the Haftorah. The reading of Maftir on the second day in the Diaspora follows the same order as on the first day.

- <u>The Haftorah</u>: The Haftorah of the 1st day of Sukkos is read from Zechariah "Hinei om Ba." The Haftorah of the second day is read from Melachim from "Vayikhalu" until "Hotziu Osam Mieretz Mitzrayim."

L. Yizkor:
- There is no Yizkor recited on the first days of Yom Tov. It is recited on Shemini Atzeres.

M. Day Kiddush:
- During the day Kiddush, the blessing of Leisheiv is said after the blessing of Hagafen, prior to drinking from the wine.

N. Preparing on the 1st day of Yom Tov on behalf of the 2nd day of Yom Tov or Shabbos:
- It is forbidden to do anything on the 1st day of Yom Tov on behalf of the next day, including on behalf of the 2nd day in the Diaspora. This applies even for the two days of Rosh Hashanah which is considered like one long day. [This applies even in a year that Shabbos falls after Yom Tov and one performed Eruv Tavshilin before Yom Tov.] This prohibition applies even against doing acts of preparation that do not contain any forbidden Melacha at all. [Rather, all the preparations for the 2nd night are to be done after Tzeis Hakochavim/nightfall of the first day. However, some Poskim rule that in a time of need, such as to prevent loss, and for the sake of a Mitzvah, one may be lenient to prepare on the first day of Yom Tov on behalf of the 2nd day, if one completes the preparation with much time left in the day, and the preparation does not involve any Melacha normally forbidden to be done on Yom Tov.]

- <u>Examples</u>: One must beware not to bring wine on the first day of Yom Tov on behalf of Kiddush of the second night. Likewise, one is not to search in a Sefer Torah on the first day of Yom Tov for the reading of the second day, or for Shabbos, even if one performed Eiruv Tavshilin. Likewise, one may not wash dishes on the first day on behalf of the second day [until after Tzeis Hakochavim]. [Likewise, one may not make the beds [or tidy the home] on the first day of Yom Tov on behalf of the next day, unless it is also done for the sake of having a clean home on the first day of Yom Tov. Likewise, one may not set the table or prepare the candles until after Tzeis Hakochavim.]

- Preparing on 1st day on behalf of Shabbos: Even in a scenario that Shabbos falls after the 2nd day of Yom Tov, it is forbidden to prepare on the 1st day of Yom Tov, on behalf of Shabbos, even when Eruv Tavshilin has been done. Rather, all preparations for Shabbos are to be done on the 2nd day of Yom Tov. Cooking with enough time so the food is ready before Shabbos: Even when Eruv Tavshilin is performed, it is only permitted to cook food for Shabbos if there is enough time for the food to be fully cooked and servable to guests on Yom Tov, prior to sunset. It is Biblically forbidden to cook foods if there isn't enough time left for the food to be served before sunset. Many are unaware of this matter.

- May one remove food from the freezer on the first day of Yom Tov on behalf of the second night meal? Some Poskim rule it is permitted to remove foods from the freezer on the first day of Yom Tov on behalf of the meal of the second night of Yom Tov. Other Poskim, however, rule that it is forbidden to remove the food even in such a case. [See footnote for opinion of Admur in this matter. Practically, it is best to avoid removing the food from the freezer until after Tzeis Hakochavim. This especially applies in light of the fact that the food can be defrosted after nightfall on top of a source of heat, and be ready for the night meal. Nonetheless, if these options are not viable and delaying the removal until Tzeis Hakochavim will cause a real delay to the meal, then one may be lenient to remove the foods from the freezer with much time left in the day of Yom Tov, so it does not appear to others that it is being done for the night.]

- May one place drinks in the fridge or freezer on the first day of Yom Tov on behalf of the second day? This follows the same dispute as above. Practically, it is best to avoid doing so unless one plans to taste the cold drinks while it is still the first day of Yom Tov, in which case it is permitted according to all.

- When are the Yom Tov candles to be lit on the 2nd night of Yom Tov? On the second night of Yom Tov, the candles are lit after nightfall, and not before sunset of the first day.

- May one prepare and do Melacha on the night of Yom Tov on behalf of the day meal? Yes.

- May one ask a gentile to prepare on the first day of Yom Tov on behalf of the second day? It is permitted to have a gentile perform preparations on the first day of Yom Tov, on behalf of the second day, so long as the action does not involve any Melacha that is generally forbidden on Shabbos. Thus, one may ask a gentile to wash dishes or sweep the floor, or set up the table, on behalf of the second day.

O. Havdalah:

- On Motzei Yom Tov, one is required to recite Havdalah over a cup of wine just like on Motzei Shabbos.

- Sukkah: A man is obligated to say Havdalah inside the Sukkah. One says the blessing of Leisheiv Basukkah after Havdalah prior to drinking from the wine.

- Haeish: During Havdalah of Motzei Yom Tov, we do not say a blessing over fire.

- Besamim: During Havdalah of Motzei Yom Tov, we do not say a blessing over Besamim.

- Nussach: The Nussach of Havdalah on Motzei Yom Tov that falls on a weekday also contains the words "Bein Yom Hashevi'i Lesheishes Yimei Hamaaseh", even though it is now in middle of the week [and it thus seems irrelevant to mention this statement]. [Thus, it follows the same Nussach as any Motzei Shabbos.]

- <u>Are the Pesukim of Hinei Keil Yeshuasi recited on Motzei Yom Tov?</u> Yes. However, some have the custom to omit it.

- <u>May one who did not say Havdalah on Motzei Yom Tov say it the next day?</u> One who did not say Havdalah on Motzei Yom Tov is to say Havdalah the next day [until sunset], and is not to eat or drink anything, besides for water, until he does so. If one did not say Havdalah the next day [prior to sunset] then he may no longer say Havdalah, and may thus continue eating and drinking as usual.

- <u>Is Vayiten Lecha recited on Motzei Yom Tov?</u> No.

3. Chol Hamoed:

A. Shemoneh Esrei-Ya'aleh Veyavo:

- One Davens a regular weekday Shemoneh Esrei for Maariv, Shacharis and Mincha, although adding Yaaleh Veyavo to the prayer. If one forgot to recite Ya'aleh Veyavo in Shemoneh Esrei he must repeat the prayer. This applies even by Maariv.

- Forgot Yaaleh Veyavo but remembered prior to finishing Shemoneh Esrei: If prior to finishing Shemoneh Esrei one remembered that he did not say Ya'aleh Veyavo, [then if he is holding prior to saying the name of Hashem in the concluding blessing of Visechezena then he should say it as soon as he remembers and continue afterwards from Visechezena. If, however, he remembered only after he already said Hashem's name in the concluding blessing of Visechezena then some Poskim rule he is to conclude the blessing with Lamdeini Chukecha and then go back and recite Ya'aleh Veyavo and then repeat from Visechezena.] If he remembered after concluding the blessing of Visechezena, but prior to Modim, then he is to say it there [and continue afterwards with Modim]. If, however, he only remembered after he already began saying Modim then he must return to Ritzei and recite from there with Ya'aleh Veyavo. If he only remembered after he already finished Shemoneh Esrei then he must return to the beginning of Shemoneh Esrei. [This applies even if he remembered after reciting the second Yehi Ratzon, prior to taking three steps.] If, however, he remembered prior to reading the second Yehi Ratzon then he is to return to Ritzei. [If he is accustomed to adding prayers after the second Yehi Ratzon, then if he remembers prior to concluding these prayers he is to return to Ritzei.]

- In doubt if said Ya'aleh Veyavo: If one is in doubt as to whether he recited Ya'aleh Veyavo then some Poskim rule he fulfills his obligation and is not required to return to Ritzei or repeat Shemoneh Esrei. Others however rule that it has the same law as one who did not say Ya'aleh Veyavo and he must hence return to Ritzei or repeat Shemoneh Esrei. Practically, one is to complete the Shemoneh Esrei and repeat Shemoneh Esrei as a Nidavah.

- If one remembered only after he already Davened Musaf: If one had already Davened Musaf and only then realized he had forgotten to say Ya'aleh Veyavo in Shemoneh Esrei of Shacharis, he does not need to repeat Shemoneh Esrei.

B. Hallel/Musaf:

- Throughout the eight/nine days of Sukkos and Shemini Atzeres, one is required to recite the complete Hallel with a blessing. See Chapter 2 Halacha H for the full details of this matter!

- The reason we say the complete Hallel on each day of Sukkos in contrast to Pesach: On Sukkos, the G-dly revelation is able to be internally felt on each day of the holiday, and thus there is an abundance of joy on each day which is expressed in the daily completion of Hallel. This ability to internalize and feel the revelation is only available after the giving of the Torah. However, on Pesach which took place before the giving of the Torah, we were unable to internalize the revelation, and thus the joy is not exorbitant enough to justify the completion of Hallel. However, on the first day of Pesach the complete Hallel is recited as we were removed from the 49 gates of impurity and there is no greater joy than this.

- The order of the Davening after Hallel: After Hallel, Hoshanos is performed as explained in Chapter 2 Halacha J. After Hoshanos, the Chazan recites Kaddish Shaleim which is then followed by Shir Shel Yom, Kerias Hatorah, Ashreiy, Uva Letziyon, and Musaf.

- Musaf: The Musaf of Chol Hamoed follows the same dialect as Musaf of Yom Tov of the 1st day of Sukkos, with exception that when the Musaf sacrifice is mentioned in the prayer, one recites the particular sacrifice of that day. The reason for this is because the Musaf sacrifices of each day of Sukkos were different than the previous day, decreasing the number of bull offerings by one each day.

- If the wrong Karban was read: If one read the wrong portion of the Karban during Musaf, he nevertheless fulfills his obligation.
- The six Zechiros: One is to recite the six Zechiros after the prayers.

C. Kerias Hatorah

- On each day of Chol Hamoed the Torah is read. One scroll is removed from the ark and the portion of the Sukkos Karbanos found in Parshas Pinchas is read from it. In Eretz Yisrael, all four Aliyos are read from that days Karban, hence repeating the same reading four times. In the Diaspora, the four Aliyos read different days of Karbanos as printed in the Siddur.
- The Chabad custom in Eretz Yisrael: The traditional custom amongst Chabad in Eretz Yisrael is to read like the rest of Eretz Yisrael, and repeat the same text four times, as ruled above. However, some Chabad congregations in Eretz Yisrael began following a similar reading to that of the Diaspora. Practically, each Rav is to direct his community in how to follow, and the community must abide by his decision. Nonetheless, it remains quite apparent that the Rebbe's final stance on the issue was not to make any changes to the accepted custom, and to read like the rest of Eretz Yisrael, repeating the same text four times.
- The number of Aliyos? On Chol Hamoed, four people are called up to the Torah. One may not call up more than four people for the Torah reading.
- Kaddish: The half Kaddish is recited after all four Aliyos are complete.

D. Rejoicing:

- It is a Biblical command for one to rejoice, himself, his wife, his children and his entire household, throughout all days of Yom Tov, including Chol Hamoed. Men are obligated to drink wine [every day of Yom Tov and Chol Hamoed] in order to fulfill their Mitzvah of Simcha. One who does not drink wine does not fulfill the command. In addition to drinking wine, there is also a [Biblical] Mitzvah, to eat meat and other delicacies, although this is not an actual obligation. [One who increases in eating other delicacies and doing other matters of joy is also considered to be fulfilling the Biblical command, although he is not obligated to do so.] One is to give his children and other young members of his household [treats such as] nuts. [Today this can be fulfilled through giving children chocolate and other candies.]
- Drinking wine: A man is to drink a Revius of wine every day of Yom Tov, including Chol Hamoed. One does not fulfill his obligation with grape juice. One can drink any alcoholic beverage. Women are not obligated to drink wine for Simchas Yom Tov.
- The meals: One is not obligated to eat any specific amount of meals on Chol Hamoed, so long as he does not fast. [Nevertheless, initially it is a Mitzvah for one to have a meal with bread. One is to eat bread twice on Chol Hamoed, once by day and once by night.] One may not fast past midday on Chol Hamoed. One must thus eat or drink something prior to midday. One is not obligated to eat specifically bread on Chol Hamoed, and it suffices even if he eats mere fruits. Nevertheless, initially it is a Mitzvah for one to have a meal with bread on Chol Hamoed, [once by day and once by night, as stated above].

E. Birchas Hamazon:

- Yaaleh Veyavo: During Chol Hamoed, one recites Yaaleh Veyavo in Birchas Hamazon. If one forgot to recite it, he does not repeat Birchas Hamazon. If he remembered prior to beginning even the first word of the blessing of "Hatov Vehameitiv" then he is to recite the blessing of Baruch Ata Hashem Elokeinu Melech Haolam Asher Nasan Moadim Liamo Yisrael Lisason Ulisimcha Es Yom Chag Hasukkos Hazeh". If one forgot to say Ya'aleh Veyavo in its set area, and he remembered only after he already began the first word "Baruch" of the blessing of Hatov Vehameitiv, then he has fulfilled his obligation, and Birchas Hamazon is not to be repeated. [He is not to recite any extra blessing on behalf of Yom Tov and is rather to continue as usual.] In such a case, it is not customary to recite Ya'aleh Veyavo in the Harachamans.
- Harachaman: Harachaman of Yom Tov is not recited on Chol Hamoed. However, Harachaman of Sukkos is recited.
- Migdol: When reciting Birchas Hamazon on Chol Hamoed, one recites "Migdol" as opposed to "Magdil".
- Meiyn Shalosh: Some Poskim rule one is to mention Yom Tov within the after blessing of Meiyn Shalosh, and so is the Chabad custom.

F. Simchas Beis Hashoeiva:

- The Simchas Beis Hashoeiva of Temple times: Chazal state that "One who did not witness the joy of the Simchas Beis Hashoeiva [in Temple times] has not seen joy in all his days." There were so many flames lit in the Temple during the Simchas Beis Hashoeiva that there was not one courtyard in Jerusalem that was not alit due to its light. Chassidim and Anshei Maaseh [Jews of high stature of fear of Heaven] would dance with torches of light, and sing various melodies. The Chassidim and Anshei Maaseh would say "Praised be our parents who did not shame our grandparents." The Baalei Teshuvah would sing "Praised be our grandparents who atoned for our parents." Both groups would say "Praised be one who did not sin, and one who sinned should repent and he will be forgiven." Raban Shimon Ben Gamliel would juggle eight torches of fire during the Simchas Beis Hashoeiva.
- The custom today: It is customary amongst Jewry to perform a joyous gathering of song and dance throughout the nights of the festival of Sukkos, in commemoration of the Simchas Beis Hashoeiva which was experienced in Temple times on this Holiday.
- The Rebbe directed that the Simchas Beis Hashoeiva should begin already on the 1st night of Sukkos and take place in the open streets.
- May an Avel participate in Simchas Beis Hashoeiva? Some Poskim rule he may only join as a spectator and may not join the dancing. Others rule he may even join the dancing however on condition that musical instruments are not being played. Others rule he may even join if there is live music playing.

G. Aliya Laregel-Visiting the Temple on a festival:

- The Mitzvah in Temple times: In Temple times, it was a Biblical command for every man to visit the Temple on Yom Tov of the Shalosh Regalim, and bring with them a Karban Olah. This Mitzvah was formally known as the Mitzvah of Reiyah, and its Karban was known as the Karban Reiyah.
- The law during exile: The bringing of the Karban is an integral part of the Mitzvah of visitation, of which without it the Mitzvah cannot be fulfilled. Accordingly, during times of

exile that we cannot bring a Karban, the Mitzvah is no longer applicable. Some Poskim however rule the Mitzvah is not dependent on the Karban, and hence the Biblical Mitzvah is simply to visit Hashem by the Temple mount area. Nonetheless, since the Mitzvah of visitation is to enter the area of the Azarah, which we cannot enter today due to ritual impurity, therefore it is not possible to fulfill the Mitzvah, even according in their opinion. Some Poskim however rule the Mitzvah is applicable even today. [Some Poskim novelize the Mitzvah can be fulfilled through seeing the floor of the Azarah, even if he is not physically there. Accordingly, some meticulous Jews of Jerusalem Jewry are accustomed during the festival to visit a high enough area to be able to see the floor of the Temple mount. Others suggest that even seeing the Kosel suffices for this regard. Other Poskim rule that although the positive command of Aliyah Laregel is not obligatory today, one who does so fulfills a Biblical obligation.] Practically, the Poskim conclude that the Mitzvah of Aliya Laregel is not applicable during exile neither from a Biblical or Rabbinical level, although remains a custom as explained next.

- The custom during exile: Even after the destruction of the Temple, the custom was to gather from all the surrounding cities of Jerusalem and visit the Temple for the festival. This is done even today. [Practically, it is Mitzvah for every person to strive to fulfill this custom.]

- For how many days does the Mitzvah apply: The Biblical Mitzvah of Aliyah Laregel mainly applied on the first day of the festival. Nevertheless, one who did not do so was able to fulfill the Mitzvah for a remaining six days, for a total of seven days. [Accordingly, one who was unable to visit the Western Wall on the first day of Yom Tov, is to do so during one of the next six days.]

- What area of Jerusalem is one to visit? The Biblical Mitzvah was to visit the area of the Azarah on the Temple mount, which cannot be done today due to impurity. The custom today is to visit the Kosel, the Western wall. Some however are accustomed to visit an area from which they can see the floor of the Temple mount, as explained above.

H. Shabbos Chol Hamoed:

- Read Haftorah of Shabbos Chol Hamoed on Erev Shabbos: On Shabbos Chol Hamoed Sukkos and Pesach one is to read to himself both the Haftorah of the Parsha of the coming week and the Haftorah which is read that Shabbos.

- Hodu before Mincha of Erev Shabbos: Hodu is omitted prior to Mincha Erev Shabbos which is also Yom Tov or Chol Hamoed. Patach Eliyahu is recited even when Hodu is omitted such as Erev Shabbos Chol Hamoed.

- Kabalas Shabbos: On Shabbos Chol Hamoed one begins the Maariv prayer from Mizmor Ledavid [psalm 29], [omitting all the Psalms from Lechu Neranina until Mizmor Ledavid]. [One recites the entire dialect from Mizmor Ledavid and onwards, including Ana Bekoach; all the stanzas of Lecha Dodi; Mizmor Shir, Kegavna. In Lecha Dodi, the wording of Besimcha instead of Berina is recited.

- Shemoneh Esrei: The Shabbos Chol Hamoed Shemoneh Esrei for Maariv, Shacharis and Mincha follows the same dialect of prayer as a regular Shabbos, with exception to that Ya'aleh Veyavo is added in the Shemoneh Esrei.

- Kiddush: On Shabbos Chol Hamoed the following passages prior to Kiddush are read in an undertone: Shalom Aleichem, Eishes chayil, Mizmor ledavid Hashem ro'i, Da Hi Se'udasa.

- Hoshanos: Hoshanos is not recited on Shabbos Chol Hamoed.

- <u>Musaf</u>: For Musaf one prays the same dialect prayed by Musaf of Yom Tov, although reciting the Shabbos additions. If one forgot to mention the Shabbos sacrifices in Musaf then if one said "Kimo Shekasuv Besorasecha" he has fulfilled his obligation. The same applies whenever one forgets to mention a particular Karban.
- <u>Kerias Hatorah</u>: Two Sifrei Torah are removed from the Ark. In the first Sefer Torah one reads the Parsha of "Rei Ata Omer Eilay." In the second Sefer Torah one reads the Maftir from Pinchas, discussing that days sacrifice.
- <u>Haftorah</u>: Both the Haftorah of Shabbos Chol Hamoed Pesach and Sukkos discuss the times of the redemption. On Pesach the Haftorah discusses the resurrection, being that the resurrection will take place in Nissan. On Sukkos the Haftorah discusses the battle of Gog and Magog, being that in Tishrei there will be the war of Gog and Magog. Thus, the Haftorah is read from the portion of "Vehaya Bayom Bo Gog" found in Yechezkel. The last blessing said after the Haftorah on Pesach concludes with only "Mikadesh Hashabbos" being that Chol Hamoed Pesach is not considered a separate Yom Tov. On Sukkos, however, it ends with "Mikadesh Hashabbos Yisrael Vehazmanim" being that each day is a separate Yom Tov.
- <u>Reading Koheles</u>: The custom is to read Koheles on Shabbos Chol Hamoed Sukkos [without a blessing]. [This is not the Chabad custom.]
- <u>Havdalah</u>: One recites Havdalah as usual for Motzei Shabbos, on Motzei Shabbos Chol Hamoed.
- <u>Is Vayiten Lecha recited on Motzei Shabbos Chol Hamoed?</u> Some Poskim rule it is to be recited. Others rule it is to be omitted. The Chabad custom is to recite it quietly.

4. Hoshanah Raba

A. The meaning of Hoshana Raba:

- During Sukkos we are judged regarding water [i.e. rain]. On Hoshana Raba, the judgment of the water is sealed. This is of significant importance to human life as human life is dependent on water.

B. Aravos for Hoshanos:

- <u>The Mitzvah</u>: On Hoshana Raba, an Aravah is taken in addition to the Aravos that are bound with the Lulav. It is taken in commemoration of the Hakafos that were performed with the Aravos in the Temple, in which the Mizbeiach was encircled with the Arava branch. These Aravos are also referred to as Hoshanos.
- A blessing is not recited upon fulfilling the Mitzvah of Aravos for Hoshanos.
- <u>Who sells the Aravos for Hoshanos</u>? The custom is for the Shamash of the Shul to sell the Aravos, just as was the custom during Temple times.
- <u>How many Aravos are taken</u>: From the letter of the law it suffices to take a single willow branch for the Aravos of Hoshanos. Some were accustomed to take two Aravos. Others would take 17 Aravos attached to one branch. Nonetheless, according to Kabbalah one is to take five Aravos and so is the widespread custom of all Jewry. [The Chabad custom is to purchase a set of Hoshanos for each family member, including one's wife and children.]
- <u>Binding the Aravos</u>: It is disputed amongst the Poskim as to whether one is to bind the Aravos together or if they are to remain loose. Practically, the Chabad custom is to bind the Aravos. However, they are not to be bound together with another species. Accordingly, some are particular to not bind them together using Lulav leaves [and rather they use another Aravah for the binding]. Practically, it is permitted to bind them together using Lulav leaves, [and so is the Chabad custom].
- <u>How many leaves must the Aravah have</u>? From the letter of the law, it suffices for the Aravah used for Hoshanos to contain even a single leaf throughout its entire branch. [Meaning, that even if all the leaves fell off, aside for a single leaf, it remains Kosher.] Nevertheless, it is degrading to use an Aravah with one leaf on one branch, and therefore the custom is to make beautiful Hoshanos, as the verse states "Zeh Keili Veanveihu."
- <u>Its length</u>: The Aravah for Hoshanos must contain the same minimum length as the Aravos used for the Lulav [i.e. 24 cm].
- <u>Other invalidations</u>: The Kashrus status of the Aravah for Hoshanos follows the same laws as the Aravos used for the Lulav [with exception to if majority of its leaves have fallen off]. [Thus, it may not be stolen, must contain at least one leaf that is not dry, cannot be cut on its top. see Chapter 2 Halacha 6!]
- <u>Using the Aravos from the Lulav for Hoshanos</u>? It is disputed if one fulfills his obligation with using the Aravos from his Lulav. This dispute only applies if the Aravos are still bound to the Lulav. If, however, one removes the Aravos from the Lulav then it is valid according to all to use them for the Aravah of Hoshanos.
- <u>Aravos of gentiles</u>: Some Poskim rule that a Jew may not cut Aravos from the field of a gentile even if he received permission from the gentile. If, however, one plans to sell it or give it to another, then he may pick it. Likewise, a gentile may pick it on behalf of the Jew.
- <u>Aravos picked on Shabbos by gentiles</u>: If gentiles [or non-religious Jews] cut the Aravos on Shabbos, as may occur when Hoshana Raba falls on Sunday, it is nevertheless permitted to

be used. Nevertheless, a Jew may not instruct a gentile to cut them on Shabbos, or instruct him to have it ready by Motzei Shabbos. If one did so, then the Aravos should not be used if the matter is public knowledge and another Aravah is available.

- May one reuse someone's Hoshanos? If there are no other Hoshanos available, one may use another person's Hoshanos.
- May one use Aravos from a used Hoshana for his Lulav? Yes.
- The Aravos ceremony: See Halacha F!

C. The night of Hoshana Raba:

- The omen of the moon on the night of Hoshanah Raba: The Rishonim record that on the night of Hoshanah Raba there is an omen in the shadow of the moon regarding all that will occur to oneself, or to one's relatives, during that year. Some write that one is not to pay any attention to this matter in order not to worsen one's Mazal. Likewise, many do not understand the matter properly and it is hence better to act with simple faith and not look into the future.
- Candles: One is to slightly increase in candles on Hoshana Raba just as is done on Yom Kippur.
- Remaining awake throughout the night: It is a custom of Jewry to remain awake throughout the entire night of Hoshanah Raba.
- The Tikkun: One is to read the Tikun Leil Hoshana Raba during the night of Hoshanah Raba. The Tikun of Hoshanah Raba consists of reading the entire Sefer Devarim [prior to midnight], followed by reading the entire Sefer Tehilim [after midnight], and passages from the Zohar selected in the Tikun. When reading Sefer Devarim before midnight one is to read Parshas Vezos Habracha as usual. It is only to be read Shnayim Mikra Echad Targum on the day prior to Simchas Torah.
- Tehillim: After midnight the entire Tehillim is read with a Minyan while wearing a Gartel. The reading is customarily not lengthy. The Yehi Ratzon for Hoshanah Raba, and for the rising of the moon is said after the reading of each of the five Sefarim. [Some also read the Yehi Ratzon for Yom Tov.]
- Apple dipped in honey: After the conclusion of Tehilim it is customary for the Gabbai to distribute apples which are to be dipped in honey and subsequently eaten in the Sukkah. This custom is applicable as well for Shuls which don't have a Sukkah as each one can eat the apple in his Sukkah at home. Before eating the apple, one should wash his hands in the same way one washes for bread. This applies to any food dipped in one of the 7 liquids.
- Immersing in a Mikveh: Those who are meticulous immerse in a Mikveh before dawn. This was the custom of the Rebbe Rashab and was also followed by the Chasidim. However, many are not careful in this.
- Marital relations: Some Poskim rule that marital relations are to be avoided on the night of Hoshana Raba [just as it is avoided on Shemini Atzeres and Simchas Torah] unless it is the night of Mikveh, or one has a very strong urge.

D. The day of Hoshanah Raba:

- Abstaining from mundane activity: It is customary on Hoshana Raba to abstain from performing mundane activities until after leaving Shul [after Shacharis]. Some are accustomed to not even carry a wallet with them [until after leaving Shul]. Now, however, the custom in some communities is to even collect money in Shul [during Shacharis] and doing so is improper.

- The dress code-Wearing a Kittle: Some are accustomed to wear a kittle on Hoshanah Raba just like is done on Yom Kippur. [It is not the Chabad custom to wear a Kittle on Hoshanah Raba.]
- Tzedakah: It is proper to add in charity on Hoshana Raba in order to sweeten the Gevuros.
- Shaking the Lulav: It is customary to remove the knots of the Lulav on Hoshanah Raba. The knots are removed only from the top part of the Lulav [by the spine]. [The Chabad custom is prior to Hallel, to remove the two upper rings which are bound on the Lulav. On Hoshana Raba one is to increase in the shaking of the Lulav and do so with great joy.]
- Shnayim Mikra: In Eretz Yisrael, one reads Shnayim Mikra Viechad Targum on Hoshanah Raba.

E. The morning prayers of Hoshanah Raba:
- Adding parts to Davening: On the seventh day which is Hoshanah Raba, it is customary [of many communities] to increase in Psalms as is done on Yom Tov. [The Chabad custom on Hoshana Raba is not to change from the regular order of a weekday Davening.] It is customary to increase in prayer and supplication on behalf of water. [These supplications are recited in the lengthy Hoshana prayers said on Hoshana Raba.]
- Hallel-Removing the knots of the Lulav: Prior to Hallel, one removes the two upper rings which are bound on the Lulav.
- Hoshanos: By Hoshanos, all the Sifrei Torah are removed and placed by the Bimah. One circles the Bimah 7 times with the 4 Minim each time saying the appropriate paragraph as printed in the Siddur. One does not circle the Bima holding the Aravos for Hoshanos.
- Hitting the Aravos: After finishing all the Hakafos and reciting the additional prayer of Hoshanos over water, one hits the Aravos five times on the ground. See Halacha F!
- Kaddish: It is customary to recite the Kaddish that follows Musaf in a Yom Tov tune. [This is not the witnessed Chabad practice.]

F. The Aravos ceremony:
- Holding the Lulav with the Aravos: It is disputed amongst the Poskim as to whether it is permitted to join the Aravos of Hoshanos to the Daled Minim at the time that he is fulfilling the Mitzvah of Daled Minim. Practically, it is proper to be stringent and not do so. Once the Mitzvah of Daled Minim is fulfilled by saying the blessing and shaking the Lulav and Esrog even one time, it may be joined. It may certainly be joined during the Hakafos, [as explained next regarding the widespread custom]. However, upon performing the hitting ritual of the Aravos of Hoshanos, one is to only have the Aravos in his hands [and not the Lulav]. There is, however, no invalidation to be holding onto other items during this time. [The above is according to Halacha, however, according to Kabbalah, one must be very careful to never join the Aravos to the Lulav anytime, and so is the practical directive. So is the widespread custom today in all places.]
- Hakafos: Some Poskim rule that one is not to perform the Hakafos around the Bima using the Aravos and is rather to circle it with only the Lulav just as was performed on the previous days. Practically, so is the proper directive and so is the ruling according to Kabbalah and so is the widespread custom today in all places.

- Some are accustomed to put down the Lulav and lift the Aravos for the recital of Hoshanos over water. According to the Arizal, however, it is only to be lifted after the entire Hoshanos is complete and Kaddish is recited. Practically, the Chabad custom is to do the entire Hakafos and recital of Hoshanos only with the Lulav, and to pick up the Aravos only after it is completed, when it is time for them to be hit.
- Hitting the Aravos: After finishing all the Hakafos and reciting the additional prayer of Hoshanos over water, then according to Halacha one hits the Aravos on the floor or on a vessel two or three times. However, according to Kabala, one is to hit it specifically on the floor and is to hit it five times to sweeten the five Gevuros. Some Poskim rule the Aravos must be hit hard enough for leaves to fall off. Many are thus accustomed to hit it on a chair and the like, in addition to hitting it on the ground, in order to make the leaves fall off. Others, however, negate this stating there is no need to remove any of the leaves, and on the contrary, the leaves are to remain intact throughout the five hits on the ground. Practically, the Chabad custom is to hit the Aravos five times only on the ground.
- Shaking the Aravos: Some Poskim rule one is also required to shake the Aravos. Practically, the Ashkenazi custom is to do both, to shake it and then to hit it. [The Chabad custom is not to do so, and it is hit without being shaken beforehand.]
- What to do with the Aravos after hitting them: Some Poskim rule that it is forbidden to benefit from the Aravos after it is used for the Mitzvah [for that entire day] unless one made a stipulation beforehand. It is, however, permitted to discard the Hoshanos of the Lulav [to the garbage] although some Poskim rule that the Hoshanos may not be stepped on. Some have the custom to save the Aravos which were hit on Hoshanah Raba and use them as fuel to burn the Chametz on Erev Pesach. Others are accustomed to save them for use of fuel to bake the Matzos. [Others are accustomed to throw the Aravos on top of the Aron. Others negate this custom. The Rebbe was not accustomed to throw the Aravos on top of the Aron. Others are particular to save the Aravos as a good omen and Segula as explained next. Based on this it is proper not to burn all the Aravos on Erev Pesach in order so some are saved for the Segula.] See Halacha 7F!
- Hitting the children with the Aravos: The custom of the Chabad Rabbeim was to gently "whip" their sons with the Hoshanah branches. This included even their adult children. Children above age 18 received three light hits. Those below 18 received one more than their age. This custom is a directive to the public. One blesses the children upon doing so that they should know of no more pain throughout the year and they should have both physical and spiritual joy.

G. The Hoshana Raba meal:

- It is customary to hold a festive meal [abiding by the limitations to be explained] on Hoshanah Rabah, after the conclusion of the prayers.
- Customarily one dips the bread in honey. As well the custom is to eat Kreplach during the meal.
- Meal limitations: On Erev Yom Tov one is to refrain from beginning a meal [of bread] past the 10th hour of the day, which is three Zmaniyos/fluctuating hours before sunset. Snacks may be eaten throughout the day, even past the 10th hour. If one transgressed or forgot and did not eat prior to the 10th hour, then he may eat a meal past the 10th hour.
- A large feast-Seudas Mitzvah: It is forbidden to eat a large meal any time on Yom Tov unless it is a Seudas Mitzvah which its date has fallen on Erev Yom Tov. In such a case, one is to

initially begin the meal prior to the 10th hour of the day and should only invite ten people besides for close relatives and the Baalei Hasimcha.

H. The Sukkah:

- <u>Diaspora</u>: In the Diaspora, it is an obligation to eat in the Sukkah even on Shemini Atzeres, as explained next, and hence the Sukkah must remain in its erect state.
- <u>Eretz Yisrael</u>: Even in Eretz Yisrael that the Mitzvah of Sukkah culminates with the start of the Holiday, one is not to take down the Sukkah until after Shemini Atzeres. There is also no need to make any changes to its structure before Shemini Atzeres, unless one plans to eat in it on Yom Tov as explained in Halacha 6B. Nevertheless, one may remove the furniture from the Sukkah starting from midday of Erev Shemini Atzeres-Simchas Torah in order to set up his home for the holiday. [Furthermore, it is implied that one is to specifically remove the furniture from his Sukkah before Simchas Torah, even if he does not need to use it at home, and so was the custom of some Gedolei Yisrael to remove the chairs and tables from the Sukkah to show that its Mitzvah has culminated.]
- <u>Entering Sukkah for last time</u>: In Eretz Yisrael, with the approach of sunset on the afternoon of Hoshana Rabah, one enters the Sukkah (and eats or drinks something there) to bid it farewell, but one does not recite the prayer of Yehi Ratzon.

I. Ledavid:

- The psalm of Ledavid is recited daily until Hoshana Rabbah, including Hoshana Rabah. [It is omitted starting from Shemini Atzeres.]

5. Shemini Atzeres:

Note for those in Eretz Yisrael: Those who keep only one day of Yom Tov [i.e. residents of Eretz Yisrael] fulfil the customs of Simchas Torah on Shemini Atzeres. See the next Halacha for the full details of the laws and customs of Simchas Torah.

A. Its spiritual meaning:

- Receive Divine service for entire year: On the day of Shemini Atzeres the entire Jewish people receive the Divine blessing and assistance for their learning of Torah and service of Hashem of the entire coming year. Just as we begin mentioning rain on Shemini Atzeres, so too we receive the spiritual rain, which is the blessing in our Divine service.
- Draws down the light of the High Holidays: During the High Holidays, we draw down revelations of G-dliness for the coming year. This is likewise drawn down during the festival of Shemini Atzeres. The only difference is in regarding the method. That which was drawn down during the High Holidays in a mode of awe and reverence is drawn down again on Sukkos, with joy and exuberance. This particularly applies during Shemini Atzeres.
- Rejoicing: It is a Mitzvah to rejoice on Simchas Torah, in all ways possible. It is the custom of the Jewish people - and hence it is Torah - to rejoice on Shemini Atzeres and Simchas Torah even more than at Simchas Beis HaShoevah, and more than on a usual Yom-Tov.
- Time is precious: The Rebbe Rayatz stated in the name of his father, the Rebbe Rashab, that the forty-eight hours of Shemini Atzeres and Simchas Torah should be dearly cherished, for at each moment one can draw bucketsful and barrelsful of treasures both material and spiritual, and this is accomplished through dancing.

B. Erev Shemini Atzeres:

- Eating a meal: See Halacha 4G!
- Taking down and removing furniture from the Sukkah: See Halacha 4H!
- Shehechiyanu by candle lighting: The blessing of Shehechiyanu is recited during candle lighting of Shemini Atzeres.

C. Eating in the Sukkah:

- Diaspora: In the Diaspora, one must eat in the Sukkah on Shemini Atzeres, by both night and day.
- The blessing of Leisheiv Basukkah is not recited when eating in the Sukkah on Shemini Atzeres.
- One is obligated to eat the bread meals and 55 grams of Mezonos within the Sukkah on Shemini Atzeres, just as is required on Sukkos itself. Regarding other foods, such as fruits, vegetables, beverages, and the like, from the letter of the law one is not required to eat them in the Sukkah, just as is the law on Sukkos itself. Furthermore, some Poskim rule that one is to specifically not eat these foods in the Sukkah in order to emphasize its lack of Biblical status. Other Poskim, however, rule that those who are meticulous throughout Sukkos to eat even fruits and drink water in the Sukkah may continue to do so as well on Shemini Atzeres. Practically, the final ruling follows the latter opinion. The Chabad custom follows the latter opinion to be meticulous even on Shemini Atzeres to recite Kiddush and eat and drink everything in the Sukkah, both by night and by day.

- Some Poskim rule that one is not to sleep in the Sukkah on Shemini Atzeres. Other Poskim, however, rule that one is obligated to sleep in it on Shemini Atzeres, just as one is obligated to eat in it. Practically, some have the custom to sleep in the Sukkah even on Shemini Atzeres, while others do not. The Chabad custom is not to do so.
- Eretz Yisrael: One does not eat or sleep in the Sukkah in Eretz Yisrael on Shemini Atzeres. Furthermore, it is even forbidden to eat/sleep in the Sukkah on Shemini Atzeres unless one makes some form of recognition that shows that the Sukkah no longer maintains its holiness and Mitzvah. For example, in Eretz Yisrael where Erev Shemini Atzeres is Hoshana Raba, one is to remove a 4x4 Tefach area of Sechach from the roofing to show that he is not intending to stay in it for the sake of the Mitzvah. See Halacha 6B!

D. The prayers:

- Is Shemini Atzeres called a Chag within the prayer liturgy? Some Poskim rule that Shemini Atzeres is not defined as a Chag/festival in the prayer liturgy. Other Poskim rule it is defined as a Chag. Practically, the final ruling follows the latter opinion to call it a Chag in the prayer liturgy.
- Hakafos: It is an ancient custom to perform Hakafos also on Shemini Atzeres just as on Simchas Torah, and to circle the Bima on the night of Shemini Atzeres seven Hakafos with the Sifrei Torah in great joy and dancing. Even after completing the Hakafos in one Shul, if one arrives to another Shul who has yet to complete the dancing, he is to join them in the dancing and rejoicing. [Practically, the Chabad custom is to perform seven Hakafos on the night of Shemini Atzeres, just as is performed on the night of Simchas Torah. See Halacha 6E for all the details regarding Hakafos! Other communities do not perform Hakafos on the night of Shemini Atzeres.]
- In Eretz Yisrael, where Shemini Atzeres and Simchas Torah coincide, the Simchas Torah Hakafos takes place during Maariv prayers.

E. The meal:

- Kiddush: The blessing of Shehechiyanu is to be recited by Kiddush. In Eretz Yisrael that Shemini Atzeres and Simchas Torah coincide, it is customary for all men to say their own Kiddush.
- Not to dip the bread in honey: On Shemini Atzeres and Simchas Torah one does not dip the bread of Hamotzi in honey.
- Marital relations: Marital relations is initially avoided on Simchas Torah unless it is the night of Mikveh or one has a strong desire.

F. Shacharis:

- There were times [in the minyan of the Previous Rebbe] when a point was made of completing Shacharis on Shemini Atzeres before midday.
- Hakafos: Hakafos is not done on Shemini Atzeres day. This applies even according to those accustomed to performing Hakafos on the night of Shemini Atzeres. In Israel, where Shemini Atzeres and Simchas Torah coincide, the Simchas Torah Hakafos takes place during Shacharis prayers. See Halacha 6!
- Torah Reading: Two scrolls are removed from the ark. The portion of "Kol Bechor" from Parshas Re'eh is read from the first Torah scroll. Five Aliyos are called up to read from the

first Torah scroll and if Shemini Atzeres falls on Shabbos, then seven Aliyos are called up. Maftir is read from the second Torah scroll, from the portion of "Bayom Hashmini Atzeres." The Haftorah is read from Melachim I 8:54-66, from Vayehi Kechalos Shlomo until UleYisrael Amo.

- In Israel, where Shemini Atzeres and Simchas Torah coincide, three Torah scrolls are removed from the ark. From the first Torah scroll one reads from Vezos Habracha until the end of the Torah. From the second Torah scroll one reads from Bereishis until the words "Asher Bara Elokim Laasos." From the third Torah scroll Maftir is read from "Ubayom Hashemini Atzeres." See Halacha 6G!

G. Yizkor:

- Yizkor is said on Shemini Atzeres. In Eretz Yisrael, Yizkor takes place after the recital of Sisu Vesimcha, prior to the recital of Ashreiy.
- No Minyan: Yizkor may be recited even if a Minyan is not present.
- Who remains in Shul? All those who have a parent which have passed away remain in the Shul. Those which both of their parents are alive are to leave the Shul.
- Candle: It is not the Chabad custom to light a candle for Yizkor. The Rebbe and Rebbe Rayatz did not light Yizkor candles.
- Aliyah: It is not the custom to be particular to receive an Aliyah on the day of Yizkor.
- How to mention the name: One is to mention the name of the Niftar together with the name of his mother during Yizkor, such as Eliezer Ben Bashe Leah. One does not mention his father's name.
- Mentioning the Rabbeim: It is customary amongst Chassidim to mention the name of the Rabbeim that they were Chassidim of in Yizkor. This has an effect on the Chassid saying it.
- Mentioning men and women separately: Men and women are to be mentioned separately in Yizkor.
- Holding on to the Eitz Chaim: The Chabad custom is to take hold of the Eitz Chaim while reciting Yizkor. This was the custom of the Rebbe Rayatz.
- Charity: One is to pledge charity during Yizkor on behalf of the soul of the deceased.
- Yizkor during the first year of Aveilus: When Yizkor is taking place during the first year of Aveilus, the mourner remains in Shul for Yizkor, although he does not recite anything while there. He is not to recite the Yizkor even quietly. One who is still prior to the first Yahrzeit, but is past 12 months of mourning, is to remain in Shul and recite Yizkor regularly. If one is within the year of one parent and past the year for another parent, then only the parent's name that is past the year is to be mentioned in Yizkor.

H. Mashiv Haruach Umorid Hageshem:

- Mashiv Haruach Umorid Hageshem is recited beginning from Musaf of Shemini Atzeres. On Shemini Atzeres prior to the silent Musaf the Chazan announces Mashiv Haruach Umorid Hageshem and it is then recited in the Musaf prayer and every prayer thereafter. See Chapter 7 Halacha 3 for the full details of this matter!
- If a person who is not praying with a different minyan heard the announcement of Mashiv Haruach Umorid Hageshem before praying Shacharis, then he should say this phrase in Shacharis as well [as in Musaf].

I. Shnayim Mikra:

On the eve of Simchas Torah [i.e. Shemini Atzeres in the Diaspora; Hoshana Raba in Eretz Yisrael] one is to read the Parsha of Vezos Habracha, Shnayim Mikra V'echad Targum.

J. Entering the Sukkah towards the conclusion of Shemini Atzeres:

In the Diaspora, with the approach of sunset on the afternoon of Shemini Atzeres one enters the Sukkah (and eats or drinks something there) to bid it farewell. It is not the Chabad custom to recite the prayer that begins Yehi Ratzon upon taking leave of the Sukkah.

K. Preparing on the 1st day of Yom Tov on behalf of the 2nd day of Yom Tov or Shabbos:

See Halacha 2I!

6. Simchas Torah:

A. Mitzvah to rejoice:

- It is customary to refer to the last day of Yom Tov as Simchas Torah. This is due to the rejoicing and festive alcoholic meals that is made in honor of the completion of the Torah.
- Rejoicing: It is a Mitzvah to rejoice on Simchas Torah, in all ways possible. It is the custom of the Jewish people - and hence it is Torah - to rejoice on Shemini Atzeres and Simchas Torah even more than at Simchas Beis HaShoevah, and more than on a usual Yom-Tov. One is not to nullify any custom which has traditionally been done for the sake of expressing joy on Simchas Torah.
- Joy of a Mitzvah and not of frivolity and aggression: The Mitzvah to rejoice on Simchas Torah is to have a true joy of a Mitzvah and not the frivolous joy that some express. Those who use aggression to express their "joy" and hence push and hit people, are not fulfilling this Mitzvah of rejoicing, and on the contrary, they cause others to distance themselves from the true rejoicing of the Mitzvah.
- Time is precious-Dance! The Rebbe Rayatz stated in the name of his father, the Rebbe Rashab, that the forty-eight hours of Shemini Atzeres and Simchas Torah should be dearly cherished, for at each moment one can draw bucketsful and barrelsful of treasures both material and spiritual, and this is accomplished through dancing.
- The joy of the Simchas Torah is a celebration of the G-dly revelation caused through the fulfillment of a custom of Jewry. The entire concept of Hakafos is a custom of the prophets and is not written of in the written Torah and was not received through oral tradition, but was rather accustomed by the prophets. This is the celebration of the connection of the Jewish people and the Torah. It is the celebration of the Torah itself, above the oral and written aspects of the Torah. Therefore, the joy of Simchas Torah far surpasses that of the Simchas Beis Hashoeiva, and all Jews are able to participate in this joy.

B. Eating and sleeping in the Sukkah on Simchas Torah:

- On Simchas Torah, one does not eat or sleep in the Sukkah. Furthermore, it is even forbidden to eat/sleep in the Sukkah on Simchas Torah unless one makes some form of recognition that shows that the Sukkah no longer maintains its holiness and Mitzvah. For example, in Eretz Yisrael where Erev Simchas Torah is Hoshana Raba, one is to remove a 4x4 Tefach area of Sechach from the roofing to show that he is not intending to stay in it for the sake of the Mitzvah. In the Diaspora where Erev Simchas Torah is Shemini Atzeres, and one is thus unable to remove the Sechach due to Muktzah, one is required to enter into it pots and pans and the like to show that the Sukkah is invalid, and its Mitzvah has completed. The above is only required on Simchas Torah, however, after Simchas Torah there is no need to make any recognition of the Sukkah's invalidation and one may continue to eat and sleep in it if he chooses, [so long as he does not intend to do so for the Mitzvah]. [The above is only required if one plans to eat or sleep in the Sukkah on Simchas Torah, otherwise there is no need for any of these recognitions to be done.]
- Removing furniture from the Sukkah: See previous Halacha regarding Shemini Atzeres!

C. The Maariv Davening:

- The Maariv prayer includes the regular Yom Tov Maariv and Shemoneh Esrei which is then followed by Kaddish Shaleim. In Chabad Shul's the custom is to now hold a Farbrengen. This is then followed by Ata Hareisa three times, Hakafos, and Aleinu.

- Increasing lights in Shul: One should increase the amount of lights in the Shul in honor of the Sifrei Torah that are removed. [In previous times this was accomplished by lighting more candles. Nowadays, one is to arrange before Yom Tov for there to be more lights than usual in the Shul.]

D. The Simchas Torah meal:

- It is customary to hold festive meals [at night and by day] with alcohol [i.e. Seudas Mishteh] in honor of the completion of the Torah. [The holding of these festivities and festive meals is very important, as it shows our joy of the Torah and elevates its honor. Those who have nullified the accustomed tradition of holding these feasts are doing a grave sin, as they have festive meals for other occasions, but for the Torah they feel no need. This is a great belittlement of the Torah.]
- Kiddush: On the night of Simchas Torah it is customary for all [men] to say Kiddush themselves. The blessing of Shehechiyanu is said by Kiddush. On Shemini Atzeres and Simchas Torah one does not dip the slice of bread in honey. On Simchas Torah one does not dip the bread of Hamotzi in honey. One is to drink wine by the meal in fulfillment of Simchas Yom Tov. It is customary amongst Chassidim to drink alcohol in order to enter one into the joyous spirit.

E. Hakafos-Dancing:

- Dancing: Although generally it is forbidden to dance on Shabbos and Yom Tov, on Simchas Torah it is permitted to dance while singing praise for the Torah, as this is in honor of the Torah.
- Hakafos: It is customary to remove all the Sifrei Torah in the Heichal by both night, by Maariv, and day, by Shacharis, and sing song and praise. Each place is to do like their custom. The custom is to encircle the Bima in the Shul, just as is done with the Lulav [during Hoshanos]. All this is done as a sign of joy. [One dances Hakafos on both days and nights with extreme joy. The Rebbe Rashab said that one draws down abundance of physical and spiritual blessing through the joy of dancing by Hakafos.]
- Hakafos may be performed even without a Minyan.
- Many are accustomed to allowing the women to come into the men's Shul to watch the Hakafos.
- Placing a candle in the Aron: Some are accustomed to place a candle in the Aron after removing the Sifrei Torah for Hakafos. Some Poskim, however, negate this custom, as it is forbidden to enter anything into an Aron other than Sifrei Torah.
- How many Hakafos to perform: Some communities are accustomed to performing three Hakafos. Other perform seven Hakafos like on Hoshana Raba. Practically, each place is to do in accordance to their custom. The Chabad custom is to do seven full Hakafos during the night dancing while at the daytime of Simchas Torah three-and-a-half circuits are made, though the text for the Hakafos is read in its entirety.
- How many Torah scrolls are removed from the Ark? The custom is to remove all the scrolls from the Ark both by night and day as stated above. [The custom is to dance also with the Pasul Sifrei Torah, and they are not considered Muktzah in this regard. Nevertheless, one may not deliberately leave a Pasul Sefer Torah in the Aron for this purpose, and hence a Sefer Torah which cannot be fixed is to be placed in Geniza. This is opposed to the general custom which allows leaving Pasul Sifrei Torah to use for Hakafos.]

- May one bring Torah scrolls from other Shuls? One may not do so as it is forbidden to bring a Torah scroll for temporary residence, although there are those who permit doing so on Simchas Torah.

- May one sit during Hakafos? In general, it is forbidden to sit when the Sefer Torah is taken out of the Aron until it is settled on the Bima. However, many are accustomed to being lenient and sit. Practically, those who sit have upon whom to rely especially if they feel weak, however those who are meticulous remain standing throughout the time, unless they are holding a Sefer Torah.

- May an Avel dance during Hakafos? Some Poskim rule it is forbidden for an Avel [within Shloshim, or within the first 12 months of mourning for a parent] to participate in the Hakafos on Simchas Torah. Other Poskim rule it is permitted for him to participate. Practically, the Chabad custom is that a mourner is not to participate in the Hakafos alone, but rather with an escort. [He is to take hold of the Sefer Torah and have another person hold his arm while encircling the Bima. Alternatively, another person takes hold of the Sefer Torah, and the Avel holds onto the Eitz Chaim while encircling.] According to all, he may watch the Hakafos from the side. If he was offered to join the Hakafos, some write that he may not refuse due to the prohibition of showing public Aveilus. A mourner may not participate in Hakafos Sheniyos in the event that music is playing. If no music is playing, he may participate with an escort, as stated above.

- Reading the Torah at night: On the night of Simchas Torah, it is customary to read the portion of Nedarim from the Torah Scroll. Each community is to follow their custom in this matter. [Practically, it is not the Chabad custom to read the Torah publicly on the night of Simchas Torah.]

- Joining the Hakafos of other Shuls: Even after completing the Hakafos in one Shul, if one arrives to another Shul who has yet to complete the dancing, he is to join them in the dancing and rejoicing.

- Resolve to spread Torah during Kerias Shema Al Hamita: It is known to all that during the reading of Shema Yisrael said in Kerias Shema Sheal Hamita of Simchas Torah, one needs to accept upon himself the resolution of dedication towards spreading Torah knowledge in a way of Mesirus Nefesh of the body, soul, and spirit. This is to be his entire essence.

- Intimacy: Marital relations are initially avoided on Simchas Torah unless it is the night of Mikveh or one has a strong desire.

F. Shacharis:

- The order of Shacharis follows a regular Yom Tov Davening until after Hallel. Kaddish Shaleim is recited after Hallel. This is then followed by a Kiddush Farbrengen, which is then followed by Ata Hareisa.

- Birchas Kohanim: On Simchas Torah it is customary for the Kohanim to recite Birchas Kohanim by Shacharis in place of Musaf. [The Birchas Kohanim by Shacharis is done with the accustomed Niggun sang by the Birchas Kohanim of Musaf of all Holidays.]

- The day Hakafos: During the day of Simchas Torah the custom is to only perform 3.5 circles around the Bima as opposed to seven. Nevertheless, all seven liturgies of Hakafos is read. Thus, one reads a single Hakafa for every half circle of the Bimah, for a total of seven half circles corresponding to the reading of the seven Hakafos. All 3.5 circles of Hakafos are performed consecutively without dancing in between or placing Sefer Torah back in Aron or even announcing "Ad Kan Hakafa...". After the conclusion of the 3.5 circles the congregation dances. At the conclusion the Sefer Torah is returned to the Aron without saying anything.

- Chitas: On Simchas Torah one is to read the Chumash and Rashi of Vezos Habracha from that days Aliyah until the conclusion of the Parsha. One is likewise to read the Chumash and Rashi of Bereishis, from Rishon until that days Aliyah. Nevertheless, one is not heaven forbid to diminish from the rejoicing of Simchas Torah in order to read the section of Bereishis and one is rather only to do so on his free time when he is in any event not involved in the rejoicing of Simchas Torah. [Thus, one who is unable to complete the learning of Bereishis on Simchas Torah due to the rejoicing is to complete it then next day on Isru Chag.]

G. The Torah reading:

- Ata Hareisa, Vayehi Binsoa and the thirteen Middos are recited prior to Kerias Hatorah, as is done on all Holidays.
- The reading and Torah scrolls: Three Torah scrolls are removed from the ark. From the first Torah scroll one reads six Aliyos from Vezos Habracha until the end of the Torah. From the second Torah scroll one reads a seventh Aliyah from Bereishis until the words "Asher Bara Elokim Lasos." From the third Torah scroll, the same Maftir as yesterday is read, from "Ubayom Hashemini Atzeres." For the Haftorah one reads from Yehoshua "Vayehi Acharei Mos Moshe." If the congregation only has two Torah scrolls then Vezos Habracha is read from the first scroll, Bereishis is read from the second scroll, and the first Sefer Torah is returned and used for the reading of Maftir. [This however only applies if the first scroll is rolled to the third Parsha prior to its Hagba. If, however the first scroll was not rolled to the third Parsha prior to its Hagba, then it is better to read the third Parsha from the second scroll.]
- Each man gets an Aliyah: It is customary to increase in calling up people for Aliyos on Simchas Torah. Practically, the custom is for every male to receive an Aliyah. To facilitate this, the Parsha is repeated many times [until Shishi, Meona Elokim Kedem]. Alternatively, many people may be called up for the same Aliyah, such as many Kohanim for the Aliya of Kohen, and many Levi'im for the Aliyah of Levi. Nonetheless, there are Poskim who question this custom. In any event, it is best when doing so that only one person says the blessing and all the others be Yotzei with him.
- On Simchas Torah relatives may be called up one after the other for Chasan Torah and Chasan Bereishis, and some say this may be done for all the Aliyos.
- If there are many Kohanim and Levi'im present, they may be given the 4th or 5th Aliyah after the regular order of Kohen, Levi and Yisrael. In such a case it is proper to repeat the order of Kohen, Levi, Yisrael.
- A Kohen or Levi may receive Chasan Torah or Chasan Bereishis.
- An Avel prior to Shiva may receive an Aliyah during Simchas Torah. However, some write he is not to be called up as one of the 5 required Aliyos.
- Kol Hanearim: It is a worldly custom that on Simchas Torah all the male children receive an Aliyah to the Torah. This Aliyah is customarily known as Kol Hanearim. [It is customary for many children to go up together. It is customary to spread a Tallis over the heads of the children during this Aliyah.] It is likewise customary to recite the Parsha of Hamalach Hagoel [after the conclusion of the reading]. [Practically, the Chabad custom is not to spread a Tallis over the heads of the children during the Aliyah of Kol Hanearim. Likewise, it is not

customary to read the verses of Hamalach Hagoel. One is to have at least one adult above Bar Mitzvah called up together with the children for this Aliyah. The adult is to say the blessings out load and have all the children listen and be Yotzei rather than have all the children say the blessing themselves. Nonetheless, some are accustomed to have all the children recite the blessings themselves. The Chabad custom is to have the adult Olah recite the blessing on behalf of all the children who cannot say it themselves. Some are accustomed to bringing their son with them for their personal Aliya rather than have the child go up for Kol Hanearim.]

- Chasan Torah/Bereishis: It is customary for the Chasan Torah and Chasan Bereishis to donate towards the Shul and arrange for a communal feast to be held. It is customary to call up even a child for Chasan Torah, and it is not necessary to give the Aliyah specially to a Torah scholar, even though there are opinions who require this to be done. [It is not the Chabad custom to spread a Tallis as a canopy over the heads of the Chasan Torah or Chasan Bereishis when they are called to the public reading of the Torah].

- Reciting Chazak Chazak Venischazek: The person who is called to the reading of the concluding passage of the Torah is to say the words Chazak, Chazak, Venischazek together with the rest of the congregation.

- Sisu Vesimcha: The prayer of Sisu Vesimcha is recited after the Maftir and Haftorah, prior to Yizkor.

- Yizkor: In the Diaspora, Yizkor is recited on Shemini Atzeres and not on Simchas Torah. See Halacha 5G!

7. *After Sukkos:*

A. Isru Chag:

- The name Isru Chag derives from the verse "Isru Chag Baavosim Ad Karnei Hamizbeiach." This means to say that this day is to be attached [i.e. Isru] to the Holiday itself, and by doing so the verse considers him to have built an Altar and sacrificed on it an offering. The Arizal taught that on the day after Yom Tov, Isru Chag, a ray of the Holiday still shines. For this reason, the following customs are relevant on Isru Chag: One is to increase a little in eating and drinking on Isru Chag. Even a Chasan and Kallah on the day of their wedding may not fast on this day. Similarly, a child may not fast on his parent's Yahrzeit.

- Some Poskim write that the customs of Isru Chag [increasing in food and drink] apply also to the night after, which is Motzei Isru Chag.

- Some Poskim rule that one is to wear Shabbos clothing on Isru Chag.

B. Tachanun:

- Tachanun is omitted from Davening from Erev Yom Kippur until the beginning of the month of Cheshvan. The prayer of Tzidkascha is not recited on the Shabbos between Erev Yom Kippur and the month of Cheshvan.

C. Mashiv Haruach Umorid Hageshem:

- <u>When does one begin to say it</u>? Mashiv Haruach Umorid Hageshem is recited beginning from Musaf of Shemini Atzeres. On Shemini Atzeres prior to the silent Musaf prayer, the Chazan announces Mashiv Haruach Umorid Hageshem. It is then recited in the Musaf prayer and every prayer thereafter.

- <u>Until when is it to be said</u>? Mashiv Haruach Umorid Hageshem is recited until, but not including, Musaf of the 1st day of Pesach. Those who Daven the Nussach of Arizal/Sephard, omit Mashiv Haruach and begin reciting Morid Hatal from the silent prayer of Musaf of the 1st day of Pesach. The Chazan thus announces prior to the silent prayer of Musaf "Morid Hatal." Those however who follow Nussach Ashkenaz still say Mashiv Haruach Umorid Hageshem by the silent Musaf of Pesach and only begin to omit it with the repetition of the Chazan of Musaf and all prayers thereafter.

- <u>If one forgot to say Mashiv Haruach-Nussach Sephard/Arizal</u>: Those who Daven Nussach Arizal or Nussach Sephard and recite Morid Hatal in the summer months, fulfill their obligation if they accidently said Morid Hatal instead of Mashiv Haruach. Even if one remembered prior to finishing the blessing of Mechayeh Meisim, he is not required to go back and recite Mashiv Haruach.

- <u>If one forgot to say Mashiv Haruach-Nussach Ashkenaz:</u> Those who Daven Nussach Ashkenaz and do not recite Morid Hatal in the summer months, do not fulfill their obligation if they omitted Mashiv Haruach. If they already concluded the blessing and began saying the next blessing [even the first word of "Ata"] they must return to the beginning of the prayer, irrelevant to where in the prayer they remembered of their omission. Similarly, if they remembered only after concluding the entire prayer, they must repeat the Davening. If one remembers prior to saying Hashem's name in the blessing of Mechayeh Meisim, then he is to say it in the place that he remembers and continue from where he left off. [If he already said Hashem's name then he is to finish the blessing and say it prior to beginning the words of the blessing of Ata Kadosh. The same applies] if he only remembered after concluding the blessing of Mechayeh Meisim but before beginning the next blessing [even the first word of

Ata], then he is to say it there. If, however, he already began even the first word of the next blessing he must return to the beginning of the prayer, as explained above.

* If one is in doubt if he said Mashiv Haruach-Nussach Ashkenaz: Those who Daven Nussach Arizal or Sephard and recite Morid Hatal during the summer, are never required to go back even if they certainly did not say Mashiv Haruach, and certainly if it is a mere doubt. However, those who Daven Nussach Ashkenaz and are in doubt if they mentioned Mashiv Haruach are to consider it as if they omitted it, if this doubt occurred within the first 30 days after Shemini Atzeres [until 22/23 Kisleiv], and hence follow the same ruling as one who omitted it.

D. Saying Vesein Tal Umatar Levracha:

* When does one begin saying Vesein Tal Umatar? Those who live in Eretz Yisrael begin saying Vesein Tal Umatar Levracha starting from Maariv of the 7th of MarCheshvan. Those living in the Diaspora begin saying Vesein Tal Umatar on the 60th day past the beginning of Tekufas Tishrei. [Practically, it is to be said from the night before the 5th of December, and in years with 29 days in February, then the year before, it is said from the night before the 6th of December.]

* Until when is it said? Vesein Tal Umatar is recited until the start of Pesach.

* Traveling to and from Israel before 5th of December: If an Israeli traveled to the diaspora before the 7th of Cheshvan it is disputed if he to begin reciting Vesein Tal Umatar on the 7th of Cheshvan in the as is done in Eretz Yisrael, or if he is to follow the area that he is currently in, and hence he does not begin to recite Vesein Tal Umatar until the 5th of December [or until he returns to Eretz Yisrael]. Practically, he is not to recite Vesein Tal Umatar in the blessing of Bareich Aleinu, but is to recite it in Shomeia Tefilla.

* One who traveled from Eretz Yisrael to the Diaspora between 7th Cheshvan and 5th December, continues to say Vesein Tal Umatar in the Diaspora. Nevertheless, if he is the Chazan, then in his repetition of Shemoneh Esrei, he is to recite Vesein Bracha as is said in the Diaspora.

* One who traveled from the Diaspora to Eretz Yisrael between 7th Cheshvan and 5th December is to recite Vesein Tal Umatar just like Bnei Eretz Yisrael. However, if he plans to return to the Diaspora before the 5th of December, some Poskim side that he is to recite it within Shomeia Tefilah.

* Forgot to say Vesein Tal Umatar: One who forgot to say Vesein Tal Umatar during the period that it is to be said, which is in Eretz Yisrael between the 7th of Marcheshvan and Pesach, and in the Diaspora between the 5th/6th of December and Pesach, the following is the ruling: [If one remembered prior to saying Hashem's name in Bareich Aleinu, then he is to say it in the place of remembrance]. If one remembered after completing the blessing of Bareich Aleinu, but prior to beginning [the first word of] Teka Beshofar, he is to say it there. If one already began saying Teka Beshofar, he is not required to return to Bareich Aleinu and rather is to say it in the blessing of Shomeia Tefilla [prior to "Ki Ata Shomeia"]. The same applies if he remembered anywhere between Teka Beshofar and Shema Koleinu. If one remembered after concluding the blessing of Shema Koleinu but prior to Ritzei, he is to say Vesein Tal Umatar and then begin Ritzie. If one remembered after beginning Ritzei but prior to taking steps back at the conclusion of Shemoneh Esrei, he is to return to Bareich Aleinu. If he already [completed Shemoneh Esrei and] took three steps back, he must return to the beginning of Shemoneh Esrei. Furthermore, even if he did not yet take three steps back but

has already recited the verse of Yihyu Leratzon at the end of Shemoneh Esrei, he must return to the beginning.

- <u>If one is in doubt as to if he said Vesein Tal Umatar</u>: If one is in doubt as to whether he recited Vesein Tal Umatar, then if he is within the 30 days from when it was begun to be said [within 30 days after the 7th of Cheshvan in Israel, and within thirty days after the 5th of December in the Diaspora] we assume that he did not say it, and it is to thus follows the same law as one who omitted it. After the passing of thirty days, we assume that he said it, and hence he is not to go back and repeat it.

- <u>If one said it prior/post its allowed time-Eretz Yisrael</u>: If one said Vesein Tal Umatar Levracha during the summer, outside of its allowed time, which is between Pesach and 7th Cheshvan [in Eretz Yisrael] or 5th December [in the Diaspora], there is a difference in law between Eretz Yisrael and the Diaspora. In Eretz Yisrael, if one said Vesein Tal Umatar after Pesach, [during the summer, which is any time between Chol Hamoed Pesach and the 7th of MarCheshvan], one is required to go back and repeat from the beginning of Bareich Aleinu. If one already concluded Shemoneh Esrei, then he must repeat it from the beginning.

- <u>If one said it prior/post its allowed time-Diaspora</u>: In the Diaspora, if one said Vesein Tal Umatar after Pesach, [during the summer, which is any time between Chol Hamoed Pesach and Shemini Atzeres], then if one is in a country that as a whole does not need rain during the summer, it follows the same ruling as Eretz Yisrael, and one must go back to Bareich Aleinu or repeat Shemoneh Esrei. If, however, one's country as a whole requires rain even during the summer months, then one who said Vesein Tal Umatar during those months is not required to go back and repeat from the beginning of Bareich Aleinu. Nevertheless, if one wills, he may repeat the Shemoneh Esrei as a Tefillas Nedava.

- If one asked for rain after Sukkos, prior to the 7th of MarCheshvan, according to Admur and other Poskim, Shemoneh Esrei is to be repeated.

- In those countries [that in general need rain after Sukkos and that's when their rain season begins], if one said Vesein Tal Umatar after the 7th of Cheshvan, prior to the 5th of December, he is not required to go back, or repeat Shemoneh Esrei. [This applies even if his country is not currently in need of rain, such as it already rained plenty, so long as it is a general time that the country needs rain. If, however, the country is not yet in need of rain, then Shemoneh Esrei is to be repeated if rain was mentioned prior to the 5th of December.] Nevertheless, if one wills he may repeat the Shemoneh Esrei as a Tefillas Nedava.

Chart for one who remembered that he did not say Vesein Tal Umatar:

Area of Shemoneh Esrei	The Law
Prior to Hashem's name in Bareich Aleinu	Say it there
Prior to Teka Beshofar	Say it there
Prior to Hashem's name in Shema Koleinu	Say it there
After saying Ritzei	Go back to back to Bareich Aleinu
After saying 2nd Yehi Ratzon	Repeat Shemoneh Esrei.

E. What is one to do with the Sechach after Sukkos?

- One is to take down the Sukkah [immediately] after Sukkos in order to show that the Sukkas construction was purely for the sake of the Mitzvah. One is not required to bury the wood used for Sechach and it may be used and benefited from for any purpose that one desires. Nevertheless, it is proper to beware not to use it for a belittling matter, as this is disrespectful to the Mitzvah that was performed with it. It goes without saying that one may not trample on the Sechach in order not to do a belittling act with it. It is proper to save the Sechach to reuse the same Sechach for the following year's Sukkah in order to reuse it for a Mitzvah purpose. If one does not desire to save the Sechach he may throw it in the garbage. However, it is proper not to place it together with all the other garbage and it is rather to be placed in a separate pile. Likewise, it is not to be discarded in an area that people walk and will trample over it. [Some have the custom to burn the Sechach used for the Sukkah in order not to use it for any other matter. This is a mere stringency.]
- It is proper not to perform a belittling matter even with the walls of the Sukkah. They are hence not to be thrown directly into the garbage. It is permitted to use them for a non-belittling use.
- It is debated amongst the Poskim as to whether the floor of the Sukkah may be used for a belittling matter during the year.

F. What is one to do with the Daled Minim after Sukkos?

- On Motzei Yom Tov, one is to take the Lulav together with the other species and place it in a special area for safekeeping. One is to place it within view as through seeing it and remembering the Mitzvah one will merit to be saved from any suffering or stress. One should not take the Daled Minim and throw them in the garbage being that they hint to a very holy and sublime matter. [Many are accustomed to save the Daled Minim until Pesach in which they are then burned together with the Chametz.]
- If one does not desire to save the Daled Minim he may throw it in the garbage. However, they are to be placed in a separate bag and only then to be placed in the garbage.

- Hadassim for Havdalah: It is proper to use the Hadassim used during Sukkos for the Mitzvah of Besamim by Havdalah, in order to add another mitzvah to its use. One is to use it together and in addition to a spice which its blessing is Borei Minei Besamim, such as clove and cinnamon. [The above, however, is not the widespread custom and many save or simply discard the Hadassim.]

- Aravos to bake the Matzos: Some have the custom to save the Aravos of the Lulav to use as fuel for baking the Matzos.

- Esrog jelly: Some are accustomed to make Esrog jelly from the Esrog of the Daled Minim. The jelly is consumed on the night of the 15th of Shevat which is the Rosh Hashanah for trees. The consumption of this Esrog jelly is a Segula for women to have an easy birth. [Some are accustomed to also save the Esrog jelly to be eaten on Shavuos.]

- The Aravos for Hoshanos: Some have the custom to save the Aravos which were hit on Hoshanah Raba and use them as fuel to burn the Chametz on Erev Pesach. [Others are accustomed to throw the Aravos on top of the Aron. Others negate this custom. The Rebbe was not accustomed to throw the Aravos on top of the Aron. Others are particular to save the Aravos as a good omen and Segula as explained next. Based on this it is proper not to burn all the Aravos on Erev Pesach in order so some are saved for the Segula.] The Aravos are a Segula for safety during travel, for being saved in a time of danger, and for being saved from fear and frightening dreams. Some write that cooking the Aravos and drinking the water is a Segula for having children.

G. Shabbos Bereishis:

- The Rebbe Rayatz stated in the name of the Alter Rebbe and in name of the Baal Shem Tov that Shabbos Bereishis, which is the first Shabbos of the year which follows the holiday season, has ability to effect one's entire year. In his words "The way one stands on Shabbos Bereishis, so is drawn onto the entire year." On this Shabbos there is a light of Chochmah which shines and this light extends to every day of the year, and all its important events, general and personal, including: Shabbos, Yomim Tovim, Hachnasas Lecheder, Bar Mitzvah's, etc. All these events receive from the light of Shabbos Bereishis. The decrees that were written on Rosh Hashanah, sealed on Yom Kippur, and packaged on Hoshanah Raba, do not leave for shipment until Shabbos Bereishis.

- On Motzei Shabbos Bereishis we pronounce "Yaakov Halacha Ledarko," that Yaakov Avinu has begun his journey.

- Some Chassidic communities are accustomed to leave the white Paroches on the Aron and Bima until after Simchas Torah, and some leave it until after Shabbos Bereishis.

H. Kiddush between 6-7:

- Some are careful to avoid saying Kiddush during the 7th sixty-minute hour past the average midday and so is the Chabad custom. In New York this is between 6:00-7:00 pm throughout the year, except for when DST is active in which case it is between 7:00-8:00. In Eretz Yisrael, this is between 5:40-6:40 pm throughout the year except for when DST is active in which case it is 6:40-7:40. Some Rabbanim however rule one is to always avoid Kiddush from 6:00-7:00 in all places. One is to recite Kiddush either prior to this time, or afterwards. Initially one is to recite Kiddush immediately upon returning from Shul and hence if he arrives home before the start of this time he should hurry and make Kiddush beforehand.

Those who are careful to avoid Kiddush during the 7th hour avoid it with all forms of wine, irrelevant of color.

יז.   הָיָה קוֹרֵא פֶּרֶק שֵׁנִי בְּרָכוֹת

ולא פריה ורביה ולא משא ומתן ולא קנאה ולא שנאה ולא תחרות אלא צדיקים יושבין ועטרותיהם
בראשיהם ונהנים מזיו השכינה שנאמר יויחזו את האלהים ויאכלו וישתו: גדולה הבטחה שהבטיחן
הקב"ה לנשים יותר מן האנשים שנא' ינשים שאננות קומנה שמענה קולי בנות בוטחות האזנה אמרתי
א"ל רב לר' חייא נשים במאי זכיין ייבאקרויי בנייהו לבי כנישתא ובאתנויי גברייהו בי רבנן ונטרין לגברייהו
עד דאתו מבי רבנן. כי הוו מפטרי רבנן מבי ר' אמי ואמרי לה מבי ר' חנינא אמרי ליה הכי עולמך תראה בחייך
ואחריתך לחיי העולם הבא ותקותך לדור דורים לבך יהגה תבונה פיך ידבר חכמות ולשונך ירחיש רננות
עפעפיך יישירו נגדך עיניך יאירו במאור תורה ופניך יזהירו כזוהר הרקיע שפתותיך יביעו דעת וכליותיך

Rav said to Rav Chiya

*"With what do women receive merit [of learning Torah]? Through escorting their children to
the Talmud Torah, and assisting their husbands in learning Torah, and waiting for their
husbands to return from the Beis Midrash"*

This Sefer is dedicated to my dear wife whose continuous support and
sharing of joint goals in spreading Torah and Judaism have allowed this
Sefer to become a reality.

May Hashem grant her and our children much
success and blessing in all their endeavors

שיינא שרה ליבא בת חיה ראשא
&
מושקא פריידא
שניאור זלמן
דבורה לאה
נחמה דינה
מנוחה רחל
חנה
שטערנא מרים
שלום דובער
חוה אסתר
בתשבע